The March of Holiness Through the Centuries

THE MARCH OF HOLINESS THROUGH THE CENTURIES

A Brief History of Holiness Doctrine

by
William S. Deal

BEACON HILL PRESS OF KANSAS CITY
Kansas City, Missouri

ISBN: 0-8341-0533-0

Printed in the
United States of America

Contents

Preface

The purpose of this book is to present the reader with a brief outline of the *biblical and historical basis for the doctrine of Christian perfection,* or entire sanctification, as it is popularly known in many churches today.

In this presentation we have purposely limited ourselves to a brief survey of the subject, in order to present a smaller book which more laymen will take time to read. We do not here attempt to "establish" this doctrine nor to "prove" its truthfulness. This has been done in larger and more critical works. It is our purpose, rather, to acquaint the reader with a brief outline of the biblical and historical foundations for the doctrine. We hope that each reader may lay this book down with a profound conviction that his belief in this great truth is grounded firmly in biblical and historical certainty.

The author is deeply indebted to the work of Rev. Walter G. Henschen, B.D., M.A., in his book *Christian Perfection Before Wesley.* After Rev. Henschen's homegoing years ago, the author prepared his own thesis on the subject, which was published and circulated for several years. It seemed to him that a new and more up-to-date presentation was now needed, hence, this book. He has drawn deeply from the work of Henschen, and hereby gratefully acknowledges his indebtedness to this work.

May God bless this message as it goes out. May it blaze its way into thousands of hearts, to bless and reassure them of the truth of this great biblical doctrine and experience.

—William S. Deal

1

Christian Perfection Defined

Before setting out on the quest of what has been the historical progress of the doctrine of Christian perfection throughout thc ages, let us look for a moment at the *definition* of this doctrine. When we have fully established the meaning and scope of the teaching we shall be in better position to trace its course through church history.

It is well known that John Wesley (1703-89) was the most outstanding proponent of this doctrine since the days of the apostles. This truth has been held in the church through the ages, but Wesley placed it into clear doctrinal perspective. To him, perhaps more than to any other person, the church owes a great debt for defining the doctrine and putting it into sharp focus.

If this sounds a bit strange, look for a moment at the great doctrine of regeneration, or the matter of being born again. This doctrine also lay largely undefined in the church for all the centuries before Wesley's time. Martin Luther developed the doctrine of justification almost to a precision point. But while regeneration is a part of the theological concept of justification, Luther said almost nothing about it. The brilliant Calvinist theologian H. A. Strong said, "John Wesley did more to develop the doctrine of regeneration than any other man since the days of the apostles."[1]

The doctrine of sanctification, on which Christian perfection is based, must rest squarely upon a satisfactory exposition and development of the doctrine of regeneration, to which it is subsequent and upon which it depends for its very existence. It was therefore necessary that Mr. Wesley first develop the doctrine of regeneration before he could properly build upon its foundation the doctrine of Christian perfection.

Mr. Wesley and his followers discovered a good foundation for their position in both the Old and the New Testaments.

In his *A Plain Account of Christian Perfection,* Mr. Wesley opens with the account of their earliest recorded definitions of Christian perfection.

> On Monday, June 25, 1744, our first conference began; six clergymen and all our preachers being present. The next morning we seriously considered the doctrine of sanctification, or perfection. The questions asked concerning it, and the substance of the answers given, were as follows:
>
> Question. *What is it to be sanctified?*
>
> Answer. To be renewed in the image of God, "in righteousness and true holiness."
>
> Q. *What is implied in being a perfect Christian?*
>
> A. The loving God with all our heart, and mind, and soul. Deut. 6:5.
>
> Q. *Does this imply that all inward sin is taken away?*

---

1. H. A. Strong, *Systematic Theology,* art. "John Wesley."

A. Undoubtedly; or how can we be said to be 'saved from all our uncleannesses'? Ezek. 36:29.

Our second conference began August 1, 1745. The next morning we spoke of sanctification as follows:

Q. *When does inward sanctification begin?*

A. In the moment a man is justified. (Yet sin remains in him, yea, the seed of sin, till he is sanctified throughout.) From that time a believer gradually dies to sin, and grows in grace.

Q. *Is this ordinarily given till a little before death?*

A. It is not, to those who expect it no sooner.

Q. *But may we expect it sooner?*

A. Why not? For, although we grant, (1) That the generality of believers, whom we have hitherto known, were not so sanctified till near death; (2) That few of those to whom St. Paul wrote his epistles were so at that time; nor, (3) He himself at the time of writing his former epistles, yet all this does not prove that we may not be so today.[2]

John Fletcher, the chief theologian of the early Wesleyan period, says in the first part of his book on *Christian Perfection:*

We call Christian perfection the maturity of grace and holiness, which established adult believers attain to under the Christian dispensation, and by this means we distinguish that maturity of grace which belongs to the dispensation of the Jews below us, and from the ripeness of glory which belongs to the departed saints above us. Hence it appears that, by Christian Perfection, we mean nothing but the cluster and maturity of the graces which compose the Christian character of the church militant.

In other words, Christian perfection is a spiritual constellation made up of these gracious stars: perfect repentance, perfect faith, perfect humility, perfect meekness, perfect self-denial, perfect resignation, perfect hope, perfect charity for our visible enemies, as well as for our earthly relations; and, above all, per-

2. John Wesley, *A Plain Account of Christian Perfection,* pp. 41-42.

fect love for our visible God, through the explicit knowledge of our Mediator, Jesus Christ. And as this star is always accompanied by the others, as Jupiter is by his satellites, we frequently use, as St. John, the phrase, 'perfect love,' instead of the word 'perfection;' understanding by it the pure love of God shed abroad in the heart of established believers by the Holy Ghost, which is abundantly given them under the fullness of the Christian dispensation.[3]

Dr. Adam Clarke, another leading theologian and commentator in the early Methodist church, is quoted by Dr. George Peck in his book on *Christian Perfection* as follows:

> The word "sanctify" has two meanings: 1. It signifies to consecrate, to separate from earth and common use, and to devote or dedicate to God and His service. 2. It signifies to make holy or pure. . . .
>
> This perfection is the restoration of man to the state of holiness from which he fell, by creating him anew in Christ Jesus, and restoring to him that image and likeness of God which he had lost . . . Sin defaced this divine image: Jesus came to restore it. . . .
>
> The word "perfection" in reference to any person or thing, signifies that such person or thing is complete or finished; that it has nothing redundant, and is in nothing defective. And hence that observation of a learned civilian is at once both correct and illustrative, namely, "We count those things perfect which want nothing requisite for the end whereunto they were instituted."[4]

Dr. Peck summarizes the doctrine as follows:

> 1. As to the nature of Christian perfection, it is clear, first, that our authors neither hold that it implies perfection in knowledge, nor a perfect fulfillment of the requirements of the Adamic law, that is legal perfection. But, secondly, that it implies simply loving God

3. John Fletcher, *Christian Perfection,* pp. 9-10.

4. George Peck, *Christian Perfection,* pp. 51-53.

> with all the heart. 2. That entire sanctification and Christian perfection are identical. 3. . . . When we design, by the term sanctification, to express the state of perfection contended for, we should qualify it by the word entire, or the like.
>
> 4. That the term perfection, signifying the completeness of a thing in the attributes of its kind, considering its circumstances and the purposes of its being, admits of various degrees. Consequently perfection varies in its character according to the character of its subject; and may vary in its degrees, in subjects of the same class, according to the circumstances of the subject, and its particular designation.
>
> 5. That by being saved from all sin in the present life, we mean, first, from all outward sin—all violations of the requirements of the law of love which relate to our outward conduct, and, secondly, all inward sin. . . . which relate to the intellect, the sensibilities, and the will.[5]

One more definition, which we think makes the Wesleyan doctrine concise and clear, is that by Bishop Foster. He says of the person entirely sanctified, that he is in

> a state in which he will be entirely free from sin, properly so called, both inward and outward. The process of this work is in this order: beginning with pardon, by which one aspect of sin, that is actual guilt, is wholly removed, and proceeding in regeneration, by which another kind of sin, that is depravity, is in part removed, terminating with entire sanctification, by which the remainder of the second kind, or depravity, is entirely removed.[6]

In a sermon, Mr. Wesley defines his meaning of perfect love or sanctification, in the following words:

> Circumcision of the heart . . . is that habitual disposition of soul which, in the sacred writings, is termed holiness; and which directly implies the being cleansed

---

5. *Ibid.*, p. 65.

6. J. A. Wood, *Perfect Love,* quoted from *Christian Purity,* p. 122.

from all sin, "from all filthiness of the flesh and spirit"; and, by consequence, the being endued with those virtues, which were also in Christ Jesus; the being so "renewed in the spirit of our mind," as to be "perfect as our Father in heaven is perfect."[7]

This was Mr. Wesley's first public declaration of his formal statement of Christian perfection. Some have claimed that toward the end of his life Wesley tended to emphasize gradual sanctification more than the instantaneous work of grace which he had taught in his early ministry. His references to infirmities being gradually overcome, and his greater tolerance toward those who disagreed with him may be partly responsible for this mistaken opinion. Mr. Wesley himself, however, claimed in his last days that he had never deviated from his earlier positions.

In his *Journal* for November 1, 1762, Wesley wrote to another exponent of holiness:

> I like your doctrine of perfection, or pure love; love excluding sin. Your insisting that it is merely by faith, that consequently, it is instantaneous, (though preceeded and followed by a gradual work), and that it may be now, at this instant. . . . I dislike the saying, This was not known or taught among us till two or three years. I grant you did not know it. You have over and over denied instantaneous sanctification to me; but I have known and taught it, (and so has my brother, as our writings show) above these twenty years.[8]

In 1766, holiness was his theme in writing to his brother Charles:

> O insist everything on *full redemption*, received by faith alone! Consequently to be looked for *now*. . . . Press the instantaneous blessing; then I shall have more time for my particular calling, enforcing the gradual work.[9]

---

7. John Wesley, *Standard Sermons*, 1:268.
8. John Wesley, *Journals of John Wesley*
9. John Wesley, *Letters of John Wesley*, 5:16.

To Freeborn Garretson, in 1785, Mr. Wesley wrote: "The more explicitly and strongly you press all believers to aspire after full sanctification, as attainable now by simple faith, the more the whole work of God will prosper."[10]

Some of Wesley's detractors assert that he never claimed the experience for himself. It is true that he was reticent about describing his own experience as a guide for others. Nevertheless, that he did profess this perfect love or sanctification seems clear from his writings. In 1744 he wrote in his *Journal:*

> I saw every thought as well as action or word, just as it was rising in my heart, and whether it was right before God, or tainted with pride or selfishness. . . . I felt such an awe, and tender sense of the presence of God, as greatly conformed me therein; so that God was with me all day long.[11]

He also recalled in his *Journal* for October 28, 1762:

> Many years ago my brother frequently said, Your day of Pentecost is not fully come; but I doubt not it will; and you will then hear of persons sanctified, as frequently as you do now of persons justified; and any unprejudiced reader may observe, that it was now fully come.[12]

Dr. George Allen Turner has well observed of Wesley as a mature man, and as the founder of the Methodist church:

> Wesley had no desire to be an innovator. He was conservative by temperament, tradition, and conviction. The last thing in which he would admit novelty was in doctrine. He thought of his work, not as a new discovery, but as a recovery of primitive Christianity. The Thirty-Nine Articles were adopted with no changes except a reduction to twenty-four. He formed

10. John Wesley, *Works of John Wesley,* 7:172. Quoted by Wood in *Perfect Love.*

11. Wesley, *Journal,* 3:157.

12. Wesley, *Journal,* quoted by B. F. Cassaway in *Entire Sanctification.*

> no article on sanctification. What he did was to draw up a code of behaviour defining the expected "fruits of repentance," resulting from "a desire to flee from the wrath to come."[13]

With these definitions of Christian perfection, we are now ready to begin tracing the story of this great doctrine. For many, Christian perfection has been normal Christian experience throughout the centuries.

---

13. George Allen Turner, *The Vision Which Transforms*, p. 217.

2

The Sure Foundation of Holiness Doctrine

Any doctrine that is to govern the lives of Christian believers in experience and conduct must be solidly based in the Word of God. When we come to examine the doctrine of Christian perfection, there is little trouble in discovering such a basis.[1]

As one examines the Bible he will discover that this truth is basic in all the Scriptures. From Genesis to Revelation, holiness is paramount. It is the stream that rises in the perennial fountain of Genesis 1:1 and culminates in the River of Life in Revelation 22. It sparkles in Eden's fountains, glows in the dazzling, mingled colors of the rainbow, flashes as fire from Sinai's glory-crowned heights, leaps from the fiery flames of every sacred altar, and is portrayed in some form in every sacrifice of the Levitical code.

---

1. For a far broader and more comprehensive study of this basic foundation, the reader is referred to Dr. George Allen Turner's *The Vision Which Transforms,* which devotes some 150 pages to this truth.

It dazzles in the fountains, babbles in the brooks, shouts from the mountain peaks of all Bible history, prophecy, and poetry. It is the seraph's note, the angel's song, and the saint's sublime theme. It is the brightest star in the Messianic promise of hope, the climaxing purpose of Christ's redemptive mission, and the central theme of His message. It is the heart of the Gospels, the backbone of the Acts, and the lifeblood of the Epistles.

Finally, it is the glorious consummation of Revelation, where one views in gorgeous panorama the sanctified saints of the ages. Standing upon the delectable mountains of Paradise, with palms of victory and harps of gold in their hands, and crowns of glory upon their heads, they praise and adore God for redemption completed in Christ.

The gifted Dr. Foster said of holiness and its place in the Scriptures:

> It breathes in the prophecy, it thunders in the law, murmurs in the narrative, whispers in the promises, supplicates in the prayers, sparkles in the poetry, resounds in the songs, speaks in the types, glows in the imagery, voices in the language, and burns in the spirit of the whole scheme from the alpha to the omega, from its beginning to its end. . . . It is the truth glowing all over, welling up through revelation—the glorious truth which sparkles, and whispers, and sings, and shouts, in all the history, and biography, and poetry, and prophecy, and precept, and promise, and prayer—the central truth of the system.[2]

Old Testament Emphasis

Any doctrine that is basic to New Testament teaching has its deep roots firmly embedded in the Old Testament. It is evident that New Testament writers were influenced by the Old Testament more than by any other factor,

---

2. Quoted from Wm. S. Deal, *Heart Talks on the Deeper Life,* p. 4.

except the teachings of Jesus, in the formulation of doctrine.

Old Testament terminology is often not precise in relation to Christian holiness as now understood. Nonetheless, the teaching is there, especially in the symbols, meanings of certain words, and the ideas which they convey.

The most important word for "holy" and "holiness" used in the Old Testament is the Hebrew word *qadosh*. It is used over 830 times. Its origin is not fully known, but it is thought to be of Semitic origin; and means to "cut off, or separate." *Qadosh* is never found except in religious usage and, so far as is now known, has no secular uses. It is synonymous with "glory," from the Hebrew *kabod,* which means "weight, honor, prestige, radiance," and generally was used to indicate the presence and power of God.

Radiance, separation, and purity seem to be the major concepts flowing from the Hebrew word translated "holy." These words are often applied to God, to men, and to things, in order to show that they are designated as set apart, or holy.[3]

Another fruitful study looks at the words in the Old Testament that refer to sin, the opposite of holiness. A frequently used term is the Hebrew word *chatta,* which means "missing the mark," or "missing the way," as in Prov. 8:36 and 19:2.

To "transgress" is another Old Testament term for sin which means to pass over a boundary into forbidden territory. The Hebrew word for this is *abar,* which also means the violation of a written commandment.

Other words as "perversity" *(avah)* and "stubbornness" *(sheriruth),* illustrate the opposite of that holiness which God demands of His creatures.[4] (See Deut. 29:19; 1 Sam. 20:30; 2 Sam. 19:19; Isa. 21:3; Jer. 3:19; 7:24.)

---

3. Turner, *Vision,* pp. 16 ff.
4. *Ibid.,* pp. 29 ff.

The Hebrew term for "perfect" *(tamim)* signifies "wholeness." It occurs 85 times in the Old Testament, 50 of which refer to sacrificial animals, meaning that they were without spot, or blemish—not diseased, but healthy. When applied to man, it carries the thought of being without moral blemish or defect.

Our word "righteousness" comes from the Hebrew *tsaddiq,* which originally probably meant "to speak the truth." But as the language developed the word came also to mean "hard, even, or straight." The varying forms of this term occur about 500 times in the Old Testament; they are applied to God and to men to designate high character. *Tsaddiq* carries a similar meaning, in many instances, to the idea of perfection referred to above.

The Old Testament uses the above words for holiness, righteousness, and perfection in relation to God. It also uses the words to indicate that God demanded these characteristics of man. Here is basic evidence that this was God's standard of life and conduct for His people. It is nowhere taught that man is to be as holy or as perfect as God. But it is implied that man is to be holy and perfect in *likeness* to God.

The use of the various words for sin also indicate that God condemns in man all that is opposite to holiness, righteousness, and perfection.

The scriptural perfection which God demands of man is, of course, not *absolute;* it is a *relative* perfection which is attainable by man through God's grace. As J. Gilchrist Lawson well says: "All that the moral law can or does require is that we should love God with all our heart, mind, strength and soul; and the Christian that loves God and his neighbor in that way is perfect, or holy, in the sight of God."[5]

---

5. J. Gilchrist Lawson, *Deeper Experiences of Famous Christians.*

Let us note two examples. In Genesis the Lord appeared to Abraham and said, "I am the Almighty God; walk before me, and be thou perfect" (Gen. 17:1). The word "perfect" here is from the root word *tamim*, and may be rendered "upright" or "sincere." From the six synonyms from this root word there are no less than 204 references, generally rendered perfect, whole, blameless, or sincere.[6]

Not only did God demand this life of Abraham, but He prefaced it by a glorious statement of His own ability to sustain Abraham in this demand. The words "Almighty God" are from the Hebrew *El Shaddai*, which means, "The All-sufficient One." The original meaning here appears to go back to nature, literally meaning, the breast of the mother. It meant, "I am your all-sufficiency; as the mother is to the suckling child, so will I be to you—all your needs supplied!"[7]

God does not demand anything but what He supplies the ability to perform in all particulars that which is required.

Isaiah was a godly young prophet. But at the end of the reign of Judah's king, Uzziah, Isaiah caught a vision of his own deeper need for cleansing. This whole scene is filled with the atmosphere of a crisis spiritual need, and of God's touch and cleansing that followed. The experience was followed by a willingness to serve God in a more perfect way. One must read the entire account carefully (Isa. 6:1-12) noting especially vv. 5-8, to get the full significance.

Some scholars feel that previous to this experience, Isaiah's prophecies had tended to be stern, harsh, and to lack love. But after God's Holy Spirit had filled and cleansed the prophet, there is seen in his very language a

---

6. Turner, *Vision*, p. 44.
7. Adam Clarke, *Commentary on the Holy Bible*, Vol. 1.

difference of attitudes—a more profound depth of love and godliness.

The New Testament Emphasis

Across the pages of the New Testament no figure among the apostles and writers looms taller than St. Paul. It was he who gave us the first systematic theology in the Book of Romans, where he formulated many of the New Testament concepts of doctrine. Paul wrote the first books of the New Testament well before the Gospels were written. It will be well, therefore, to start our brief survey with his work.

As in the Old Testament, words again play an important role in describing the doctrines of man's salvation and of the standards of grace and perfection which God demands of man.

As in the Old Testament, "holy" signified the moral character of God and the standard of perfection which God requires of man, so in the New Testament the word signifies the same truth. It comes from a Greek root, *hagios*. From this root word come at least five other terms, all dealing with separation from sin and dedication to God. These words are: *holy, saint, sanctify, dedicate* and *consecrate,* together with their derivatives such as sanctify, sanctification, holy, holiness, etc. As Pope has well said:

> The terms which belong to this branch of Christian theology . . . constitute the largest class of homogeneous phrases in the New Testament. . . . They embrace the entire vocabulary of the Altar, its sacrifices, oblation, and priesthood, Divine and human; sanctification, dedication, presentation, hallowing, consecration; sprinkling, washing, and putting away sin; purity, sanctity, love, and holiness, and with opposites of these with all their shades; sealing, anointing, and therefore,

> the very word Christian itself. . . . The careful discrimination of their meanings . . . is the best method of studying this whole subject.[8]

A study of the above words in the New Testament reveals that in almost all instances, they are, in some manner, applied to the believer to indicate his separation from sin and dedication to God. In many instances they indicate an experience of cleansing from sin, and a sealing to God by His Spirit in the peculiar manner reserved for those who are "sanctified and made meet for the master's use"—for those who are "made perfect in love." For a more detailed study of these words in relation to Christian perfection, see Turner's work on this subject.[9]

The *prayers* of St. Paul furnish another clue to his idea of perfection as related to believers. For the Colossians he prayed that they might be "holy and unblameable and unreproveable in his sight" (Col. 1:22). Such unqualified goals for Christian life could be reached only in the perfect love of the sanctifying experience.

Note Paul's prayer for the Thessalonians: "The very God of peace sanctify you wholly; and I pray God your whole spirit and soul and body be preserved blameless unto the coming of our Lord Jesus Christ" (1 Thess. 5:23). This prayer is prayed as a present possibility. Paul knows that the experience can become a reality here and now, and remain a continuing relationship with God throughout the life of these believers.

For the Ephesian Christians, the apostle prays that they may be "filled with all the fulness of God" (Eph. 3:19), while for the Philippians he asks that they may be "filled with the fruits of righteousness" (Phil. 1:9-11).

Jesus himself appears to teach a second crisis in His words to the multitudes: "Come unto me . . . and I will give

---

8. W. B. Pope, *A Compendium of Christian Theology,* 3:28.

9. Turner, *Vision,* pp. 114 ff.

you rest; take my yoke upon you and learn of me, and ye shall find rest unto your souls" (Matt. 11:28). Here we have two rests. The first is a rest given to the sinner. When he comes to the Savior—a rest from guilt, and from the bondage of sin. The second rest comes through full commitment to discipleship, and is *discovered* along the way—"Ye shall *find* rest."

In the original Greek there are different words used here for rest. The first is a verb form meaning to "pause," and to "refresh one's self," as when the traveler stopped at the ancient well side. The second rest is translated from a noun form of the word, and means literally, "to take up habitation"; "to settle down." This term signifies the complete rest of spirit that comes to the believer when he is cleansed from sin and given the Holy Spirit as a Comforter for life. In this light, Charles Wesley sang of this verse.

Let us all in Thee inherit,
Let us find that second rest.

On the great feast day Jesus cried: "'If any man is thirsty, let him come to Me and drink. He who believes in Me, as the Scripture said, "From his innermost being shall flow rivers of living water"'" (John 7:37-38, NASB).[10] John adds his comment: "This spake he of the Holy Spirit, which they that believe on him should receive: for the Holy Ghost was not yet given; because Jesus was not yet glorified" (v. 39).

Christ also prayed for the sanctification of His followers. He wanted them to be conformed to the likeness of God and of himself so that they might become one with the Father and the Son (John 17:17-21). The twofold purpose of this sanctification is here said to be: (1) That they may be one with the Father and the Son, and (2) That this one-

---

10. *New American Standard Bible* © The Lockman Foundation, 1960, 1962, 1968, 1971, 1972, 1975. Used by permission.

ness—the Christlikeness of the believer—might convince worldly people of the truth of Christ's mission to save men.

Here is the heart of the redemptive work of God in Christ. It was intended to so draw men to God that their lives would show forth the likeness of Christ and the love of God the Father, who in Christ, was "reconciling the world unto himself."

The New Testament Church opens with the obedience of the apostles and disciples of Christ following His admonition to "tarry ye in the city of Jerusalem until ye be endued with power from on high" (Luke 24:49).

Pentecost, as recorded by Luke in Acts 2, was the fulfillment of Christ's promise to send the Holy Spirit to His believing followers (John 16:7-16; 17:17-21). This outpouring of the Spirit filled the followers of Christ with power to witness and to spread the gospel; without this enduement, there would have been no real success of the Early Church. Note the refilling and refreshing of the Spirit, and the increase of the souls won to Christ not long after the original Pentecost (Acts 4).

Further note should be made of Philip's revival at Samaria and of the consequent sending of Peter and John to minister to them. When these brethren came and found the converts rejoicing in Christ, they laid hands on them and prayed for them that they "might receive the Holy Ghost." Although they had been converted to Christ, as yet the Holy Spirit had "fallen on none of them" up to this time (Acts 8:1-15). Here the crisis experience of the baptism with the Spirit clearly followed the conversion of these Samaritan disciples.

Likewise, Cornelius and his household, received the Holy Spirit when Peter preached to them. They were God-fearing people, and appear to have been in a state of regeneration. Peter later reported this experience of Cornelius to the apostles at Jerusalem. He testified that their hearts had been "purified by faith," even as his and others had been at Pentecost (Acts 15:8-9).

The 12 disciples at Ephesus represent another group who seem to have been enjoying fellowship with God before they were baptized with the Spirit. In Acts 19:1-7, we read that Paul prayed for them and they received the Holy Spirit.

All these examples strengthen the evidence that the doctrine and experience of Christian perfection by sanctification and the Spirit's infilling are found in the New Testament Scriptures as well as in the Old.

This, then, is the foundation of the biblical teaching of Christian perfection. As we study the evidence available, our assurance grows that the ideal of Christian perfection rests squarely upon a broad and solid base in both the Old and New Testaments.

Despite the clear teachings of Scripture, the church has not always seen this truth, nor proclaimed it clearly. But this should not surprise us when we recall that *all* the cardinal doctrines of the church—including regeneration and justification by faith, as well as entire sanctification—have suffered eclipse when the church has sunk low in spiritual condition.

The loss of the ideal of Christian perfection was no more unusual than the loss of a true understanding of justification until Luther's time. Just as the Reformers revived the doctrine of justification by faith, so John Wesley brought back to the attention of the church the cardinal doctrine of the entire sanctification of believers and their infilling with the Holy Spirit.

In the chapters ahead we turn our attention to those who kept alive this gracious doctrine of Christian perfection in the church. And we shall see how it sprang to the attention of the church almost universally with the dawn of Wesley's day.

3

The Ante-Nicene Fathers

This period covers roughly the time between the earliest of the Church Fathers, Clement of Rome (ca. A.D. 30), and the Council of Nicea, which adjourned about A.D. 325. There is abundant evidence that Christian perfection was taught by these Early Church Fathers.

The Custom of Laying on of Hands

Most Bible scholars and commentators as well as most church historians are agreed that it was a custom of the Early Church to lay their hands on believers and pray for them to be filled with the Holy Spirit. The usual order was first to baptize the converts to Christianity, then the elders would lay hands upon them, praying for them to receive the gift of the Holy Spirit. So far as we have any scriptural record, this was first practiced by Peter and John at Samaria. Philip had won many new converts there, and when the two apostles came from Jerusalem, they laid their hands on them, praying that the Holy Spirit would be given to them (Acts 8:14-17). In the case of the Ephesian disciples, Paul also followed this custom (Acts 19:1-6). This is probably the practice that is referred to in Heb. 6:2 as one of the foundation principles of the gospel.

At Pentecost, and at the baptism of Cornelius's household with the Spirit, there was no laying on of hands. Some think that at Pentecost this may have been due to the fact that there were no previously Spirit-filled believers to perform this ministry. It was not done at the house of Cornelius because it was not until after that time that Jews would lay hands on Gentiles for this purpose. However this may have been, it is clear that the early order in the Church was first conversion, then baptism, then the laying on of hands to receive the Holy Spirit.

One authority says:

> The laying on of hands in prayer was a very ancient custom, and the early Christians probably adopted it from the Jews. . . . The custom of laying hands on ministers when ordaining them is practised in the churches today. . . . The Greek church and other Eastern churches, the Roman Catholic church, the Lutheran church, the Church of England, and a few smaller churches, still retain a relic of the old apostolic custom in what they call Confirmation services, although it is to be feared that these services are often little more than a mere form. In the confirmation services of all these churches the bishops, or priests, lay hands on the persons confirmed and pray for them to be filled with the Holy Ghost. The mere form, however, amounts to but little unless the Holy Spirit actually comes to dwell within. If He does this either with or without the laying on of hands, there will be new life and power in the experiences of the Christian.[1]

This doctrine of Christian perfection is woven into the earliest literature of the Church Fathers. It appears in the

---

1. Lawson, *Deeper Experiences,* pp. 45 ff.

"Memoirs" of Justin of the apostles, and in the writings of Clement of Rome. Both lived just after apostolic times, and echo New Testament ideas. As Dr. Turner has noted, "The phraseology of Paul, of I John and of I Peter is woven into exhortations to brotherly love as the highest expression of the Christian life."[2]

The Witness of the Church Fathers

The writer following the apostles who is considered as the first of the Church Fathers was Clement of Rome. He is believed to have been a very young man, just starting into the ministry with St. Paul at Philippi when the church was founded. His early testimony, therefore, is significant: "Let us then beg and pray of his mercy that we may be found in love, without human partisanship, free from blame. . . . Those who were perfected in love by the grace of God have a place among the pious" (I Clement, L., 2-3).[3]

In another early writing, is the following passage which testifies to the ideal of Christian perfection: "Their lot is cast 'in the flesh', but they do not live 'after the flesh'. . . . They obey the appointed law and they surpass the law of their own lives. . . . 'They are abused and give blessing'" (Epistle to Diognetus, V. 8-15).[4]

And from the same Epistle come the following words on the possibility of Christian perfection, "Do not wonder that it is possible for man to be the imitator of God; it is possible when he will."[5]

Both Greek and Roman Early Christian Fathers testify to the fact that it was customary for Christians to be filled with the Spirit when they were prayed for, just as

---

2. Turner, *Vision.*
3. Kirsopp Lake, *The Apostolic Fathers,* 1:95.
4. *Ibid.,* 2:361.
5. *Ibid.,* 2:373.

they had been in Bible times. Tertullian, a second-century writer, says it was common for the believers to be anointed with oil, before praying for them to be filled with the Holy Spirit. The oil being a symbol of the Spirit, as it was often understood to be in the Scriptures.

In his book on *Baptism,* chapter 6, Tertullian says: "The baptized, when they come up out of the bath, are anointed with oil, then the hand is laid upon them with the invocation of the Holy Spirit."[6] In the same book, chapter 3, he also says:

> After baptism, the hand is imposed, by blessing, calling and inviting the Holy Spirit; then that Holy Spirit willingly descends from the Father upon the bodies that are cleansed and blessed. . . . In baptism we do not receive the Holy Ghost, but being cleansed by baptismal water, we are disposed for the Holy Spirit under the hand of the minister.[7]

In his *Epistle to the Corinthians,* Clement says:

> By love were all the elect of God made perfect. . . . All the generations from Adam unto this day are passed away; but those who were made perfect in love are in the regions of the just, and shall appear in glory at the visitation of the kingdom of Christ.[8]

That praying for the Holy Spirit to come upon the believer was no mere form is evident from the writing of Irenaeus, about A.D. 150. He tells us that in his time, "when God saw it necessary, and the Church prayed and fasted much, they did miraculous things, even of bringing back the spirit of a dead man."[9]

Early Christian writers seem to have often referred to the Spirit's filling of a believer as "the Lord's seal" or "The Lord's signature," probably because anointing with oil was

---

6. See Tertullian, *Ante-Nicene Fathers.*
7. *Ibid.*
8. Clement, *Ante-Nicene Fathers.*
9. Lawson, *Deeper Experiences,* pp. 51-52.

often used in this ceremony. The idea of the "seal" may have come from Paul's term "sealing" (Eph. 1:13), and have referred to the time when they were sealed with the Spirit (Acts 19).

Eusebius, the Early Church historian, relates a writing of Clement of Alexandria, about the close of the second century. Clement told how the apostle John delivered a young man to the care of a bishop. After baptizing him, the bishop "sealed him with the Lord's signature, as with a safe and perfect guard" (Book III, chap. 17).[10]

Origen, a leading Church Father, about A.D. 210, in his *Seventh Homily on Ezekiel,* says:

> The unction of Christ, of holy doctrine, is the oil by which the holy man is anointed, having been instructed in the Scriptures, and taught how to be baptized; then changing a few things he (the minister) says to him, "Now you are no longer a catechumen, now you are regenerated in baptism; such a man receives the unction of God."[11]

Firmilian, writing also in the third century, quoted by Cyprian in Epistle 75, compares St. Paul's "confirming" of the Ephesians (Acts 19) to the confirming of the people in his own time. Firmilian and St. Ambrose seem to be among the first to use the word "confirm," or "confirmation," to describe the laying on of hands in prayer for the Holy Spirit. The term doubtless is derived from Paul: "Now he which stablisheth [or confirmeth as it is rendered in the ancient Latin versions] us with you in Christ, and hath anointed us, is God; who hath also sealed us, and given the earnest of the spirit in our hearts" (2 Cor. 1:21-22).

In the time of St. Ambrose the Latin word *confirmatio,* which means confirmation, or establishing, began to

10. See Eusebius, *Ante-Nicene Fathers.*

11. See Origen, *Ante-Nicene Fathers.*

be the common word for describing imposition of hands in prayer for the Holy Spirit. The Holy Spirit does confirm, or establish, people; and the word confirmation is a good word to describe the filling of the Holy Spirit; but the word has been used so much to describe what is often a mere form or ceremony administered sometimes by wicked and corrupt popes, cardinals, and bishops, that it has lost much of the simplicity and power of its meaning.[12]

Ignatius, who was martyred around A.D. 110-17, wrote in his *Epistle to the Ephesians:*

> Nothing of this is hid from you, if ye have perfect faith in Jesus Christ, and love, which are the beginning and the end of life: faith is the beginning, love the end; and both being joined in one are God. All other things pertaining to perfect holiness follow. For no man that hath faith sinneth; and none that hath love hateth any man.[13]

St. Ambrose (ca. 370), in his book on *The Sacraments,* chapter 2, calls the reception of the Holy Spirit through imposition of hands and prayer, "a spiritual seal remaining after baptism that perfection may be had."[14]

In *The Ecclesiastical Hierarchy,* generally attributed to Dionysius the Areopagite, and possibly written around A.D. 600, there is a passage in chapter 2 on how prayer was offered for the baptized, that they might receive the Holy Spirit. Further on it is stated, "But even him who is consecrated in the most holy mystery of regeneration, the perfect unction of chrism gives him the advent of the Holy Spirit."[15]

Jeremy Taylor, learned bishop of the Church of England, explained in his *Discourse on Confirmation,* that the imposition of the hands in prayer for the Holy Spirit

---

12. Lawson, *Deeper Experiences,* pp. 53 ff.
13. Ignatius, *Ante-Nicene Fathers.*
14. Ambrose, *Ante-Nicene Fathers.*
15. *Ibid.*

came to be known as the "Sacrament of Chrism." He says: "It was very early in the church that to represent which was ministered in confirmation, the unction from above, they used oil and balsam, and so constantly used this in their confirmation that from that ceremony it had the appellation."[16]

Irenaeus, writing in the second century, says of Paul's threefold blessing in prayer for the sanctification of soul, body, and spirit:

> How then, indeed, did he have the cause of these three, . . . unless he knew the common salvation of *these* was the renovation of the whole three? Wherefore he calls those *perfect* who present the three faultless to the Lord. Therefore those are perfect who have the spirit and perseverance of God, and have preserved their souls and bodies without fault.[17]

But of all the fathers, Macarius, the Egyptian, writes most specifically and consistently upon Christian holiness. He, in his *Homilies,* treats the subject of set purpose. He says:

> One that is rich in grace, at all times, by night and by day, continues in a perfect state, free and pure, ever captivated with love, and elevated to God. . . . In like manner Christians, though outwardly they are tempted; yet inwardly they are filled with the divine nature, and so nothing injured. These degrees, if any man attain to, he is come to the perfect love of Christ, and to the fullness of the Godhead.

He further states:

> As iron, or lead, or gold, or silver, when cast into the fire, is freed from that hard consistency which is natural to it . . . after the same manner the soul that has renounced the world, and fixed its desires only upon the Lord, and hath received that heavenly fire of the God-head, and of the love of the Spirit, is disen-

16. Lawson, *Deeper Experiences.*
17. *Ibid.*

tangled from all love of the world, and set free from all the corruption of the affections. . . . For when the soul is thoroughly cleansed from all its corrupt affections, and is united with an ineffable communion to the Spirit, the Comforter, and is thoroughly mixed with the Spirit, and is become spirit itself; then it is all light, all eye, all spirit, all joy, all rest, all gladness, all love, all bowels, all goodness, and clemency. . . . being blameless within and without, and spotless, and pure; for being brought to perfection by the Spirit, how is it possible that they should outwardly produce the fruits of sin? Sin is rooted out by the coming of the Holy Spirit, and man receives the original formation of Adam in his purity. . . .

What, then, is that "perfect will of God" to which the apostle calls and exhorts every one of us to attain? It is perfect purity from sin, freedom from shameful passions, and the assumption of perfect virtue; that is, the purification of the heart by the plenary and experimental communion of the perfect and divine spirit. To those who say that it is impossible to attain unto perfection, and the final and complete subjugation of the passions, or to acquire a full participation of the Good Spirit, we must oppose the testimony of the divine scriptures; and prove to them that they are ignorant, and speak both falsely and presumptuously.[18]

Wesley was especially influenced by Macarius and included a portion of the *Homilies* in his Christian Library, vol. 18.

Clement's *Exhortation to the Heathen,* his *Instructor,* and the *Stromata,* are among the most valuable ancient works that have come down to us, in which are clearly set forth the steps from the new birth onward to Christian perfection.

In an article published in the *Free Methodist,* January 22, 1932, on "Entire Sanctification, A Biblical, Historical and Experimental Fact," No. 2, H. A. Baldwin refers to

---

18. *Ibid.*

Wesley's *Journal* (March 4, 1769) as follows: "Wesley says that it was the reading of the remarkable description of a perfect Christian given by Clement of Alexandria which inspired him to write his tract, 'The Character of a Methodist.'"

Just after the middle of the second century (ca. 160-80), Montanus rose to considerable heights of popularity in the Church. He attracted to his following two outstanding ladies—Prisca and Maximillina—who became "prophetesses." Montanus mourned the loss of power in the Church, and claimed to be inspired by the Paraclete (from the Greek, *Paracletos,* for Comforter—Teacher) to prophesy to the multitudes the will of God for them. This movement grew rapidly and spread over a great part of the Early Church.

At first it was a simple movement calling the Church back to revival and old-time purity and power. It attracted considerable attention by the fact that in its wake many women arose as preachers. Much emphasis was placed upon the work of the Holy Spirit and His abiding presence in the heart and life of the believer. Prophecy became an outstanding part of the movement, and some of its adherents ran into extremes of fanaticism. Montanism was finally condemned as a heresy by the church leaders and lost its power as time passed.

Tertullian, who flourished around A.D. 175-220, became one of the most outstanding voices of Montanism. He, far more than Montanus, led the better part of the movement. Dr. C. F. Wimberly described Tertullian as an outstanding personality, "intelligent, devout, and sincere"; a leader in what today would have been called "the Holiness Movement."[19] We have already seen quotations from his book on *Baptism,* which illustrate how much reference was

---

19. C. F. Wimberly, *Beacon Lights of Faith.*

made to the work and place of the Holy Spirit in Christian living in that day. Tertullian was finally excommunicated from the church for his stand with the Montanists and for his refusal to denounce their position. However, he is regarded today by both Catholics and Protestants as one of the most outstanding of the Church Fathers.

As Turner points out, there arose early in the church the ideal of perfection through human suffering. This reached its peak in the idea that martyrdom was a final means through which Christian perfection might be achieved. In some quarters a shift developed from simple trust in Christ for the coming of the Holy Spirit and perfect love. The doctrine spread that we attain this Christian perfection through suffering and self-renunciation.

An illustration of the heights to which this mistaken idea led was the martyrdom of Polycarp (ca. A.D. 180). He actually begged that nothing be done to keep him from suffering for his Lord. This emphasis on perfection through works grew in the Roman Catholic church throughout the centuries. Even Wesley, in his earliest days, is seen to have been influenced by it in his desire to go to Georgia as a missionary "to save my soul, and to flee from the wrath to come."[20]

As the centuries passed, the ideal of Christian perfection shifted from the apostolic teaching of obtainment through faith, manifested by love in the life, to one of attainment by works, manifested in contemplation and a life of separatism. Out of this mistaken ideal grew the monasteries and the various orders with their monks, friars, and nuns. One of the most outstanding examples of such a life and its possibilities was St. Francis of Assisi. He was, of course, not a typical example. For the most

---

20. Turner, *Vision,* pp. 164-65.

part, the followers of the monastic movements never reached anything like his spiritual excellence.

These references, however, certainly show that the ideal of perfection, as originally taught by Christ and His apostles, was never totally lost sight of by the church in these centuries.

4

The Great Controversy on Perfection

Pelagius was a brilliant British monk who flourished during the last part of the fourth century and well into the first part of the fifth.

About the dawn of the fifth century Pelagius's teachings on the freedom of the will and on grace as the gift of God to all men came to the attention of Augustine, one of the most outstanding of the Church Fathers. Augustine lived in northern Africa and flourished about A.D. 385-430.

Pelagius affirmed that all men are born with free wills and that all have in them a divine spark of God's grace that may be fanned into a flame of love for God. He denied that any man lived sinlessly without being born again. In his earlier days, however, he seems to have claimed that a life of sinlessness was obtainable by man without the necessity of conversion, particularly where one had been brought up to know and accept the grace of God in early life.

Augustine, who had led a wicked life until his conversion in his mid-20s, had been under the influence of various ethical philosophies from which he had tried to find the good way. He was strongly influenced for a while by Manichean dualism—the idea that human nature is essentially sinful because it is material. He was also influenced by similar views in Neo-Platonic philosophy. Augustine's Christian experience and background of training led him immediately to reject Pelagius's ideas about man's free will and the nature of grace.

Here we rely upon the work of Walter G. Henschen in his book *Christian Perfection Before Wesley,* and his quotations showing the development of this controversy and its outcome.

Dr. George Peck says:

> Pelagius maintained that the will is naturally free to do good, and is not at all impaired by the fall; that there are no special influences of the Spirit in regeneration, but all the helps that are necessary in that work is instruction, and that man can by this aid perfectly keep the law. . . . Pelagius was brought before a council of fourteen bishops belonging to Palestine, at Diospolis, (Lydda,) A.D. 415, to answer to sundry charges. Charge VI is, "Pelagius has said that man may be without sin." To this Pelagius responds, "I have indeed said that man may be without sin, and keep God's commandments, if he will. For this ability God has given him. But I have not said that any one can be found, from infancy to old age, who has never sinned, but being converted from sin, by his own labor and God's grace he can be without sin; still, he is not by this immutable for the future."[1]

The same writer quotes from Professor Wiggers as follows:

> Augustine himself, in his earliest writing against the Pelagians, (De Pec. Mer. II, 6; De Spir. et Lit. 1,) had granted, nay, even defended, the position, (taken in the abstract as the Pelagians took it,) that, by God's grace, man can be without sin. And though he did not

---

1. Peck, *Christian Perfection,* pp. 90-91.

himself believe, that anyone is without sin in this life, (De Pec. Mer. II, 7,) still he did not regard this as a dangerous opinion, provided only that one does not believe we can attain it by our own power. (De Spir. et Lit. 2; De Nat. et Gr. 60.) I know this is the opinion of some, (viz., that there have been, or are, men without sin,) whose opinion in this matter I dare not censure, though I cannot defend it, (De. Perf. Just, Hom. 21.) In the letter of the five bishops to Innocent, as well as in several of the early pieces of Augustine, this position was left doubtful, or at least pronounced a sufferable error. . . . Even Ambrose had held to it, in a certain sense. And in his book on the Acts of Pelagius, c. 30, written soon after, Augustine numbers this question, both in the abstract and in the concrete, among those which are not to be denied as though already decided in opposition to the heretics, but to be kindly discussed among the Catholics. But, after this synod, (in C. d Epp. Pel. IV, c 10,) he represents this opinion as a dangerous and detestable error. He does not, however, here present it in the abstract sense in which the Pelagians really held it, but as if they maintained that there were and had been righteous men who, in this life, had no sin. And from this time onward, as appears from C. Jul IV, 3, he could not endure the doctrine of man's ability to be without sin (*Historical Presentation,* p. 174).

Peck adds:

It should be carefully considered that the perfection for which Pelagius contended was a *legal perfection*—perfect conformity to the demands of the law of innocence. It also appears that he entertained the notion that "the grace of God is given according to our merits"—that "the merit of good-will precedes grace." He says: "When man is divinely aided, he is aided for the purpose of attaining perfection. The nature of man is good which deserves the aid of such grace."[2]

2. *Ibid.*, pp. 189 ff.

A careful examination of these positions will convince an unprejudiced mind that the system is but little understood. Too frequently Pelagianism is charged upon those who are even farther from that heresy than those who bring the charge. It will have been observed that Augustine sometimes denies, and at other times admits that men can live without sin. Hence both those who assert and those who deny the doctrine of perfection often quote him as authority.

Henschen, who has furnished the principal part of my materials upon the Pelagian controversy, advertises of a change in the opinions of Augustine as to the possibility of keeping the law, after the Council of Carthage. But as early as this period, the distinction between mortal and venial sins, which occupies so prominent a place in Romish theology, had obtained. And Augustine held this to be a catholic verity.[3]

Farther on in his discussion of the question, Peck summarizes a treatment of the subject by Bishop Jewell, in which Peck says, "These fathers evidently, after all their zeal against the Pelagian error of perfection, acknowledge —as all, indeed, who reverence the Scriptures are forced to do—a qualified perfection to be predicable of men on earth."[4]

To the same point, Rev. H. A. Baldwin contributed a series of illuminating articles in the *Free Methodist* on the subject, "Entire Sanctification, A Biblical, Historical, and Experimental Fact." In Part 3, January 29, 1932, Baldwin has this to say regarding Augustine and Christian perfection: "In his early writings Augustine acknowledged that one might be made holy. His change of mind came about in this way: Augustine always taught that membership in

3. *Ibid.*, pp. 96, 98.
4. *Ibid.*, p. 108.

the orthodox church was a necessity to salvation. When the Donatists dissented from the orthodox church, because of its declining spiritually, Augustine attacked them with great bitterness."

One of the leading tenets of the Donatists was Christian perfection. In fact, Wesley once said the Donatists were the Methodists of their day. Augustine was the kind of man who could not oppose a movement for a supposed wrong and at the same time acknowledge any possible right. Christian perfection must, therefore, be rejected along with the errors of the Donatists. The departure of Augustine from the doctrine of perfection was completed in his savage onslaught on Pelagius, whom he accused of teaching that man could by his own will make himself holy. Pelagius denied this charge, but the denial made no change in Augustine's opposition. Wesley says that as far as he could discern, Pelagius was one of the holiest men of his day.

That Augustine at one time acknowledged the possibility of holiness is seen in the following question posed 10 years after his conversion and years before the Pelagian controversy: "Can it at any time or place be an unrighteous thing for a man to love God with all his heart, with all his soul, and with all his mind, and his neighbor as himself?" (*Confessions*, Book III, Chap. 8).

In his book *On the Forgiveness of Sins* (Book II, chap. 7), Augustine acknowledges the possibility of living without sin, but denies that any person has succeeded in so doing. A friend, Marcellinus, was much disturbed by such a statement and wrote Augustine to this effect. Augustine replied by writing his book *On the Spirit and the Letter*. In the book he restated his proposition and added that any who thought they could attain to such a height without the grace of God were in error. Nevertheless Augustine adds, "If, however, anybody . . . shall have proved that some man or men have spent a sinless life upon earth, whoever does not, not merely refrain from opposing him, but also does not rejoice with him to the full, is afflicted with extraordinary goads of envy" (chapters 1—3).

In his book *On Man's Perfection in Righteousness,* chapter 21, Augustine states that there were some whose views he did not have the "courage to censure" who believed that sinlessness was a possible experience.

Augustine occupies the unenviable position of being the first among the Church Fathers to come out squarely against the doctrine of deliverance from inward sin. John Fletcher calls him the "father of rigid imperfectionists."

In his book *On the Spirit and the Letter,* chapters 65 and 66, he states that there is no man living on the earth "who is absolutely free from all sin." His argument in this place amounts to, "God can, but will not." In this connection he also states that no man can hope in this life to attain to the fullness of love enjoyed by those on the other side. But Augustine concedes that a man can reach a place in his life where he will be swayed by no lust.

These citations sufficiently illustrate the confusion that existed in the mind of this great man with reference to the doctrine of Christian perfection.[5] One of the great tragedies of church history is that Pelagius and Augustine were never privileged to meet face-to-face. Being the kind of men both of them were, had they met and formed a solid acquaintance and possibly some sense of friendship and better understanding, they may have resolved their differences in a far different manner than they did.

There are three periods in Augustine's life, properly speaking—early, middle, and late. In his early period Augustine held essentially the views that the church had held through the preceding centuries. Even in the middle

---

5. W. G. Henschen, *Christian Perfection Before Wesley.*

period he is not so far gone from the historic position of freedom of the will with free grace and salvation for all men. It is essentially in his late period that he goes so far astray from the genuine message of the New Testament. In this period he departed from the Fathers into what later became known as Augustinian theology, and finally, as we know it today, extreme Calvinism.

John Calvin in the sixteenth century revived and somewhat refined Augustinianism, giving to Protestantism what we now know as Calvinistic theology. Augustine, in his stubborn fight against Pelagius, to defend what he felt was the truth about grace and salvation, swung far over to the extreme positions he espoused. In the formation of his final theology, Augustine embraced elements of both Neo-Platonism and traces of the old Manicheanism. These views are reflected in his rejection of the human flesh and many normal pleasures of life as being utterly sinful.

Augustine's position, while approved by the church as correct in rejecting Pelagianism at the time of the controversy, was never accepted by the entire Church as its true position. Martin Luther, as an Augustinian monk, saw when he first attempted preaching these tenets to the public masses, that his message would fall on deaf ears and become a failure. As Luther progressed in his prosecution of the Reformation ideals, he swung back to the historic position of the church—free grace for all men, salvation for all who will accept it, and damnation only for such as persist in their sins to the end of life. The early Reformation was essentially a move back toward the ideal of Christian perfection by faith, not by works, as the apostles had taught.

5

Christian Perfection in the Pre-Reformation Era

During the Middle Ages, when well-meaning, pious souls wanted to get away from the world of corruption in the Roman Catholic church, many of them formed various orders and adopted plans and methods by which they tried to cultivate holy living. Among these different orders were groups known as the "Mystics," some of whom no doubt attained to a high degree of piety and holiness.

One may not approve of some of their ascetic practices, but their earnest desire and effort to live a holy life is to be commended. There can be no doubt about the earnestness and sincerity of many of them of whom God certainly took note and gave them "the desire of their heart." We believe the promise was fulfilled to them which says, "Blessed are they which do hunger and thirst after righteousness: for they shall be filled" (Matt. 5:6).[1]

1. Henschen, *Christian Perfection*.

The place occupied by the Mystics of the Middle Ages in forwarding the truth of Christian perfection was very succinctly stated by Bishop J. Paul Taylor, in the *Free Methodist* for December 4, 1932, on the subject, "Holiness —the Doctrine of Antiquity."

He writes:

> For some years before Wesley's time the holy waters had been gliding silently through the homes and assemblies of the Mystics in England, the Pietists in Germany, and the Quietists in Spain, Italy and France. It was from such sources that Wesley first "caught the singing of the waters." There were some foreign elements of a dangerous tendency in the teachings of these groups, but a perfect process of filtration took place, as the truth poured through the capacious soul and discerning mind of the great founder of Methodism.

In his book on *Scriptural Sanctification,* Dr. John R. Brooks comments as follows on the wonderful baptism of the Holy Ghost received by the devout and distinguished church historian Merle D'Aubigne.

> Here indeed was a most blessed experience; but not something strange and exceptional in religious biography. We can trace the same thing under different names through many saintly lives. The "inward death" of Mysticism; the "divine stillness" of Quietism; the "rest of faith" of the Brethren of the Higher Life—all these terms are readily translated back into the one idea of the peace of God ruling in the heart. It is, in a word, the perfect quiet which comes to the soul that is yielded up in perfect self-surrender to God. Tauler is constantly describing it as the fountain of that wonderful second life of his after his two years' retirement from the pulpit into the cell. "If man truly loves God," says he, "and he has no will but to do God's will, the whole force of the river Rhine may run at him and will not disturb him or break his peace."[2]

---

2. John R. Brooks, *Scriptural Sanctification,* pp. 219-20.

John Tauler himself, whose life of purity and powerful preaching were a rebuke to his age, left a clear witness. He writes that the possessor of the life of Christian perfection enjoys "the most quiet and peaceful liberty, being uplifted above all fear and agitation of mind concerning death and hell, or any other things which might happen to the soul either in time or in eternity."[3]

There were other men of the Middle Ages and Pre-Reformation times who kept alive the great truth of Christian perfection. They did so more by the lives they lived and the examples they set than by direct teachings.

Thomas à Kempis

Born in 1380, Thomas à Kempis was destined to wield a powerful influence over the Church before his sun finally set in death in 1471.

The best known work of à Kempis is *The Imitation of Christ*. This work leans somewhat toward Christian perfection through works, suffering, and renunciation. Yet there are in it unmistakable traces of that striving for perfection which has always been the golden ideal of the saints. The book does not emphasize a definite crisis experience, but there are glimpses of the idea that this grace and blessed fullness of Christ are to be had by faith in Him.

This prayer of à Kempis reveals something of the utter dedication of the man and of his trust in God for complete guidance in all things: "Give what thou wilt, and how much thou wilt, and when thou wilt. Send me where thou wilt, and deal with me in all things as thou wilt."

Girolamo Savonarola

Girolamo Savonarola, of Italy, was one of the greatest reformers, preachers, prophets, politicians, and philoso-

---

3. *Ibid.*, pp. 220 ff.

phers the world has known. His public career as a preacher began the same year that Luther was born. Someone has said that if the soil of Italy had been as congenial as that of Germany to a Protestant Reformation, he, instead of Luther, might have been the instrument in God's hands for that Reformation. As it was, Savonarola was the precursor of the Reformation. By his terrific denunciation of the corruptions of the Catholic church, he prepared Europe for Luther's work.

Savonarola was born in Ferrara, Italy, September 14, 1452, of cultured but worldly parents. At an early age he became a diligent student, and afterwards attained great proficiency in the liberal arts and in philosophy. He was an earnest student of Aristotle, but the writings of the great Greek philosopher left Savonarola's deepest longings unsatisfied. The philosophy of Plato gave him a little more satisfaction; but it was not until he began to study the writings of Thomas Aquinas that he found real food for his soul. It was doubtless the writings of that great saint which led Savonarola, at an early age, to yield his whole heart and life to God. The works of Aquinas probably continued to influence his life more than any writings outside of the Scriptures.

As a boy, his devotion and fervor led him to spend many hours in prayer and fasting. Disgusted with the corruption of the age, he decided to enter the monastic life of a Dominican convent, which he did April 24, 1475. Here he fasted and prayed, led a silent life, and became increasingly absorbed in spiritual contemplation. Soon after entering the convent he was made a lecturer on philosophy to the monastery, which position he held during the remainder of his years there.

In 1481 Savonarola went to the convent of St. Mark's in Florence, the most beautiful and cultured city in Italy. It was the city where he was to become famous. Here the

Renaissance (revival of learning) had affected the life of the people more than in any other place. One year after entering the convent, Savonarola was made instructor of the novices, and finally raised to the rank of preacher in the monastery. Although the monastery had a splendid library, he came more and more to use the Bible as his textbook. He was filled with a sense of approaching judgment, terror, and the vengeance of God, and often gave voice to this message when sent to preach in the neighboring towns. But his preaching had so little effect either in Florence or the surrounding towns, that he decided to give up preaching and confine himself to teaching the novices.

In 1482 Savonarola was sent to Reggio d'Emilia, there to represent his convent in a Dominican chapter-general. During the first day, while the monks were discussing dogma, he remained silent. But on the second day when a question of discipline came up, he arose and in powerful accents denounced the sins and corruption of the church and clergy. His soul was stirred and he spoke with an eloquence that made a profound impression. Returning to Florence he could not refrain from preaching. But his sermons still made little impression on the pleasure-loving Florentines.

It was about this time that Savonarola had an experience with God that revolutionized his life and ministry. In prayer and meditation he waited upon God, yearning for a direct revelation from Him. One day while engaged in conversation, he received a vision. The heavens opened, the future calamities of the church passed before his eyes, and he seemed to hear a voice charging him to announce these truths to the people.

This was apparently Savonarola's Pentecost. From that moment he was convinced of his divine mission, and was filled with a new unction and power. His preaching was now with a voice of thunder, and his denunciation of sin became terrific. The people who listened to him sometimes went about the streets bewildered, speechless, and half-dazed. His congregations were often in tears, so that the whole church resounded with their sobs. Men and women of every age and condition—workmen, poets, philosophers—would burst into passionate tears. Pico della Mirandola tells of a sermon of Savonarola's which "made a cold shiver run down his back, and made his hair stand on end."

The preacher's ardor for prayer, his faith, and his devotion increased day by day. His companion, Fra Sebastiano of Brescia, says that Savonarola, when engaged in prayer, frequently fell into a trance; he was sometimes so transported by holy fervor that he was obliged to retire to a solitary place. His biographers relate that on Christmas eve, in the year 1486, Savonarola, while seated in the pulpit, remained immovable for five hours, in an ecstasy; his face seemed illuminated to all in the church, and this occurred several times afterward.

Savonarola told his friend and biographer, the younger Pico della Mirandola, that on one occasion while meditating on the text, "Blessed art Thou, O Lord; teach me thy statutes," he felt his mind illuminated, and all doubts left him; he felt more certainty of the things that were shown him than a philosopher did of first principles.

In 1484, Savonarola was sent as Lenten preacher to the little republic of San Gimignana. Here he preached with such power that he returned to Florence with greater confidence in his mission. He was later sent to preach in various cities of Lombardy, especially in Brescia. Everywhere he went, his denunciations of sin awakened a holy alarm, and his fame continued to spread over Italy.

In 1489, when he returned to Florence, the Lord revealed to him that great things awaited him there. He began to explain the Book of Revelation to the friars in the garden of St. Mark's convent. But his fame had spread through Florence until laymen begged for admittance to his lectures. His congregations increased daily until he had to move to the sanctuary and lecture from the pulpit of the church.

The church was thronged for the first service, and many stood or clung to the iron gratings in order to see and hear the preacher. The voice of Savonarola seemed to have an almost superhuman effect, and the audience was raised to a transport of ecstasy. After that service, all Florence spoke of Savonarola, and even the most learned flocked to hear him.

By Lent of 1491, San Marco church had become too small to hold the people, and Savonarola moved to the famous Duomo, the cathedral church of Florence. Here he remained during the final eight years of his preaching in Florence. The people were so eager to hear him that they arose in the middle of the night, and waited hours for the cathedral doors to open. They came along the street singing and rejoicing. They listened to his sermons with such interest that when they were finished the people thought they had scarcely begun. Savonarola seemed to be swept onwards by a might not his own; and he carried his audiences with him.

The people of Florence abandoned their vile, worldly books, and instead read Savonarola's sermons. All prayed and went to church. The rich gave freely to the poor, and merchants restored ill-gotten gains amounting to many florins. Even the street gamins stopped singing ribald songs, and sang hymns instead. All the people forsook the carnivals and vanities in which they had indulged; they made huge bonfires of their masks, wigs, worldly books, and obscene pictures. Even children marched from house to house in procession, singing hymns, and collecting everything they styled vanities. These they carried to the bonfires amidst singing of hymns and pealing of bells.

But the triumph of Savonarola was short. During his first sermon after returning to Florence, he predicted that he would preach there only eight years. He also foretold his own martyrdom. Although people from all over Italy flocked to Florence to hear him, his fearless sermons aroused the anger of many. The hierarchy of the church—the corrupt pope, cardinals, and priests—were furious. Savonarola was threatened, excommunicated, and persecuted. Finally, in 1498, by express order of Pope Alexander VI, he was burned to death in the public square of Florence, the city he loved so well. His last words were, "The Lord hath suffered so much for me." Thus perished one of the world's greatest saints and martyrs.[4]

John Wyclif

John Wyclif, an Englishman who died about 1384, wrote a volume entitled *Of Perfect Life*. Dr. George Peck, in his *Christian Perfection*, quotes the following paragraph from it:

> To be turned from the world, is to set at naught, and to put out of mind, all likings, joys, and mirths thereof, and to suffer meekly all bitterness, slanders, and troubles thereof, for the love of Christ, and to leave all occupations unlawful and unprofitable to the soul, so that man's will and thought be dead to seek anything that the world seeketh and loveth. Therefore the prophet speaketh in the person of the soul's *perfectly* turning to God, saying, Mine eyes, that is my thought and intent, shall ever be to God. For he shall draw my feet, that is my soul and affections, out of the snare, and the net of the love of this world. He that is truly turned to God, fleeth from vices, beholdeth not the solaces or comforts of this world; but setteth his mind

4. Lawson, *Deeper Experiences*.

so steadfastly on God, that he well nigh forgetteth all outward things; he gathereth himself all within; he is reared up wholly unto Christ.[5]

Erasmus

Desiderius Erasmus, a Dutch scholar and churchman, was born in Rotterdam in 1492. He never left the Roman Catholic church, but his scholarly work in Bible languages gave impetus to Reformation influences.

Dr. George Peck quotes Erasmus's comments on Matt. 5:8 ("Blessed are the pure in heart: for they shall see God"):

> How much more blessed be they who, being delivered from blindness of the mynde, have the gift inwardly to see God. As the sunne is to cleare eyes, so is God to pure and cleane mindes. As matter of skumme or a webbe is to the eyes, so is God to the pure and cleane mindes. Therefore, blessed be they whose heart is *pure and cleane from all filthyness.* For they shall have this gift, which is more to be desired than all the pleasures of the world: they shall see God. [This paraphrase was translated by order of Henry VIII into English, and ordered to be placed in the churches.][6]

These sketches show that right up to the eve of the Protestant Reformation the idea of the holy life was known and encouraged by many within the church.

5. Peck, *Christian Perfection,* pp. 70-71.
6. *Ibid.,* p. 71.

6

Christian Perfection and the Reformation Leaders

The very necessity for the Reformation was brought on by the loss from sight of the great evangelical doctrines of the Church. These doctrines had given Christianity power and force in the world for centuries. They had not in reality been lost from the Church so much as they had been covered over with a mass of ceremonialism. They had lost their place and power in the lives of people through failure to proclaim them.

Luther did not intend to promote a revolt from the church, but rather to produce a *revival within it.* The Reformation came because the church leaders refused to go along with the genuine revival that Luther sought to kindle. The ceremonialism and the hardness of the unregenerate hearts of the church's leaders resisted the call for reformation and renewal. Luther and his movement were literally expelled from the church.

The Reformation was both a *moral and spiritual necessity;* without it the work of God would doubtless have fallen into total decay. The church could have in time become a wholly pagan institution, with only traces of vital Christianity left within her.

The main burden of the Reformers was to revive the doctrine of justification by faith and to deliver the church from a mere form of worship embedded in its rituals and ceremonies. The Reformers sought a return to a simple, direct worship of God "in spirit and in truth."

It seems that it was the work of Luther, in the providence of God, to revive the doctrine of justification; and it was the work of Wesley to revive the doctrine of sanctification or Christian perfection. The church in the time of the early Reformers was hardly in adequate spiritual condition to receive a renewed emphasis on the teaching of a higher life.

The Reformers did their work well; they fulfilled their mission. They rescued the fundamental evangelical doctrine of justification by faith; they restored the Scriptures to and for the masses; they broke down superstition and ritualism; they purified the church of corruption—all of which was a necessary preparation for the renewed call to the higher life of entire sanctification and holiness.

Although both Luther and Calvin were influenced by Augustine's doctrine of imperfection, yet at times they reflected concern for the essential elements of Christian holiness. In an editorial in the *Herald of Holiness,* May 25, 1932, Luther is quoted as saying in connection with his definition of the church, "They are called a Christian people, and have the Holy Ghost, who daily sanctifies them, not only by the forgivenss of sin, but also by the laying aside, expelling and destroying of sin, and hence they are called a holy people."

It is clear that the Augsburg Confession, and its great defender, direct their opposition, not against the Wesleyan theory of evangelical perfection, but a *graceless* theory of Pelagians, and the *legal* system of the Romanists.

Dr. Peck says:

> The only passage in the Augsburg Confession which has any reference to the subject under discussion is the following: "They condemn the Pelagians, and others, who teach that it is possible, by the sole power of reason, without the aid of the Holy Spirit, to love God above all things, and do His commandments."[1]

The expressions of Reformer Melancthon upon the subject of the remaining corruptions of the "regenerate" are not a whit stronger than those of Mr. Wesley, which he gives us in his sermon on "Sin in Believers." The difference seems to be that Mr. Wesley makes a *general,* and Melancthon a *universal* application of his doctrine to the actual state of Christians.

In addition to their Confession of Faith, the Reformers submitted to the Diet a list of corruptions that had crept into the Roman church—corruptions which they had corrected. Chap. 6, "Of Monastic Vows," contains the following explicit statement of the doctrine of Christian perfection:

> Those therefore who would be justified by their vows, have abandoned the grace of God through Christ; for they rob Christ of his glory, who alone can justify us, and transfer this glory to their vows and monastic life. It is moreover a corruption of the divine law and of true worship, to hold up the monastic life to the people as the only perfect one. For Christian perfection consists in this, that we love and fear God with all our heart, and yet combine with it sincere reliance and faith in Him through Christ: that it is our privilege and duty to supplicate the throne of grace for such things as we need in all our trials, and in our respective callings, and to give diligence in the performance of good works. It is in this that true perfection consists, and the true

1. Peck, *Christian Perfection,* p. 116.

worship of God, but not in begging, or in a black or white cap.[2]

The *Theologia Germanica* which Luther prized so highly gives the following stages by which the soul attains unto perfection:

A. The purification concerneth those who are beginning or repenting, and is brought to pass in a threefold wise:
   1. By contrition and sorrow for sin;
   2. By full confession;
   3. By hearty amendment.

B. The enlightening belongeth to such as are growing, and also taketh place in three ways, to-wit:
   1. By eschewal of sin;
   2. By the practice of virtue and good works,
   3. And the willing endurance of all manner of temptation and trials.

C. The union belongeth to such as are perfect, and also is brought to pass in three ways, to-wit:
   1. By pureness and singleness of heart;
   2. By love,
   3. And by the contemplation of God, the Creator of all things.[3]

This discussion may be fittingly concluded with a prayer adopted by the Reformers: "Cleanse the thoughts of our hearts by the inspiration of the Holy Spirit, that we may perfectly love Thee, and worthily magnify thy holy name, through Jesus Christ our Lord."

Such a prayer, insofar as it was authentic and typical, reveals a yearning for that perfection which all saints sincerely desire. That it came out of the period of the Reformation on the continent of Europe, reflects the awakening of a deep spiritual concern among the churchmen of that time.

---

2. *Ibid.*, pp. 116ff.
3. *Theologia Germanica,* chap. 14, art., "Purification" (numbering mine).

The Scottish Reformers

The work of Saint Patrick early in the Christian centuries had left an impress for holiness upon the Scottish mind in general. Although the church had sunk into corruptions and a morass of ceremonial anemia, there was left in the Scottish consciousness some kind of yearning for better days. It was to this mass consciousness that the early Reformers of that land appealed.

As would naturally be expected the Scottish reformers were influenced by Augustine's theology. But there were also expressions of concern for the higher life that reflected a trend toward Wesleyan theology. This is shown by James Alex McDonald in his *Wesley's Revision of the Shorter Catechism.* After stating in his preface that Wesley was influenced by Scottish piety, among other things through Henry Scougal's *Life of God in the Soul of Man,* he says, "This 'Life of God in the Soul of Man' is the essence of true Christianity. It is the secret of Pentecost. . . . This experience of perfect love has not been unknown to many of our most useful Scottish saints, among whom it was sometimes called the 'rest of faith,' 'the full assurance of faith.'"

McDonald also quotes from Patrick Hamilton these words, "He that loveth God keepeth all His commandments. He that hath faith keepeth all the commandments of God," and then adds, "Wesley's work was twofold. By preaching justification by faith he reaffirmed the Reformation doctrine. . . . Preaching entire sanctification by faith he reaffirmed and developed the early Reformation doctrine of Holiness as maintained by Patrick Hamilton."[4]

Another significant statement regarding Wesley and the *Shorter Catechism* appears in McDonald's preface:

---

4. James A. McDonald, *Wesley's Revision of the Shorter Catechism,* p. 85.

As far as we can judge, there is but one sentence in the whole Confession (1560) which Wesley's followers might wish to improve—the work of the Holy Spirit, in the sanctification of believers, should have a fuller expression, such as Knox has himself admitted, by incorporating the "Places" of Patrick Hamilton in his History of the Reformation. It appears to us that Hamilton has expressed in a most thoroughgoing manner the doctrine of holy living, which was the secret of the great Methodist revival.

Robert Blair, one of the founders of the Presbyterian Church in Ireland, is quoted in *Scot's Worthies* as saying,

> I perceive that many who make a right use of faith in order to attain unto the knowledge of justification make no direct use of it in order to sanctification. And that the living of the just by faith reacheth further than I formerly conceived, and that the heart is purified by faith. I had not learned to make use of faith as a means and an instrument to draw holiness out of Christ. . . . I saw it was no wonder this occasioned an obstruction in the progress of holiness and I perceived that making use of Christ for sanctification without directly employing faith . . . was like one seeking water out of a deep well without a long cord to let down the bucket and draw it up again.[5]

5. *Ibid.*, pp. 190 ff.

7

Christian Perfection and the Arminians

Martin Luther swung away from the harsh theology of Augustine, where salvation was by election, and that to be worked out by God alone. He moved to a more balanced position, in which God and man cooperate in man's salvation, and free grace is seen to be for all. This was the historic position of the Church, and there was no stir caused by this turn away from Augustinianism.

However, with the rise to prominence of John Calvin, at Geneva, Switzerland, in the 16th century, Augustinianism was revived and considerably refined. Calvin reworked Augustine's doctrine into a powerful new system of theology, and presented it to the world in his famous *Theological Institutes.* This Calvinistic statement took deep roots in the minds of multitudes and soon those who accepted this view of theology were in the leadership of the Reformation in central Europe.

During this period, Jacobus Arminius, a brilliant Dutch theologian at the University of Leyden, was asked to write a treatise in defense of Calvinism against those who had dared to express contrary views. After long and careful research, Arminius discovered that he and others had been misled in their Calvinistic views. It was clear that Augustine and Calvin had built a theological system upon a complete misunderstanding of biblical passages dealing with "group election and predestination." They had twisted these passages into an unscriptural "individual predestination" that was not even known in the church prior to Augustine's time.

With this discovery, Arminius, with great conviction, proceeded to correct Calvinism. He sought to bring men back to the scriptural position of freedom of the will, grace for all men, and salvation, not by election, but by faith and perseverance in that faith to the end of life.

This revival of biblical truth caused a storm of protest and controversy. That, of course, is another story. However, every informed believer owes it to himself to read the *Life and Works* of Jacobus Arminius. He should know what Arminianism teaches about the freedom of the will and salvation by faith, as opposed to the Calvinistic idea of election.

Arminius

Arminius and his colaborers in the seventeenth century were charged by an opponent, Gomarus, with holding "the perfection of men in this life." This charge called forth from Arminius a specific statement of his views. Dr. Peck says of this statement, "It seems, he did not profess to differ from the *earlier and more sober views of* Augustine upon the subject." Arminius had said:

> Besides those things of which I have already spoken, much has often been said concerning the perfection of believers, or the regenerate, in this life, and it is reported that I hold views on this subject which are improper, and almost the same as those of the Pelagians, viz., that the regenerate can in this life perfectly observe the precepts of God. To this I reply, that I

ought not, on this account, to be considered either partially or wholly a Pelagian, even if I held this view; provided that I should make this addition—that they could do this by the grace of Christ, but by no means without it. Yet I have never said that a believer can in this life perfectly observe the precepts of Christ, nor have I ever denied it, but have left it entirely undetermined.[1]

Episcopius

Episcopius was the brilliant successor of Arminius in the divinity chair at the University of Leyden. In private discussions with pupils in Amsterdam, he was given a series of questions to answer. One of these had to do with his concept of perfection:

> Quest. 19. "Be ye therefore perfect even as your Father which is in heaven is perfect" (Matt. 5:48). The question is, "What should be understood here by the word perfect? Is it that we should perfectly keep all the commands of God and Christ without any sin, (except those which preceded conversion)? But if so, whether this is necessary for attaining to the life of the blessed."

The answer of Episcopius was, in part, as follows:

> Embracing the opportunity afforded by this question, I wish also to answer another—"Whether a man, assisted by divine grace, can keep all the commands of God, even to a perfect fulfillment, that is, using the word love in a general manner for keeping the commandments, whether he can love as much as he ought to love according to the requirement of the gospel, or according to the covenant of grace?" I, indeed, have no doubt on this point.
>
> My reasons are these: 1st. God demands no other love than that which is rendered by the whole mind, the whole heart, and all the strength. Therefore he demands nothing beyond or above the strength. 2nd. God promises that he will circumcize the heart of his people, that they may love Him with their whole heart

1. Peck, *Christian Perfection,* p. 132.

and mind. (Deut. 30:6). 3rd. God Himself testifies that there have been those who have kept all His commands all the days of their life with their whole mind, and heart, and strength, and this in the sight of God: as we may read of Asa, (1 Kings 15:14); of the whole people, (2 Chron. 15:12); of David, (1 Kings 11:34, and 14:8, and 15:11); of Josiah, (2 Kings 22:2); that he "Turned to the Lord with all his heart, and with all his soul, and might, according to all the law of Moses," (2 Kings 23:25). And we read that these things were attributed to them by God under the old covenant. Who, then, can doubt that the same thing can have place in the new covenant?

The common distinction between a perfection of parts and one of degrees requires explanation. . . . But if by a perfection of degrees is understood that highest perfection which consists in the highest exertion of human strength assisted by divine grace, and which is joined with the purpose of making continual progress in proportion to his increased strength, then I believe there is no reason why it should be said to be impossible to man on the earth. . . .

The highest evangelical perfection (for we are not treating of legal perfection, which includes sinlessness entire in all respects . . .) embraces two things:—1st. A perfection proportioned to the powers of each individual; 2nd. A desire of making continual progress, and of increasing one's strength more and more. This perfection varies in respect to beginners, proficients, and those perfect in the knowledge of divine truth, and of that love which is required of us: for which reason there is one perfection higher than another, or the perfection of some is higher than the perfection of others.[2]

Limborch

Dr. Peck quotes from the learned Limborch, another able follower of Arminius, on this same subject:

The possibility of keeping the commandments of our Saviour is taken for granted by what has been said

2. *Ibid.*, pp. 134 ff.

of the necessity thereof; since things necessary must be observed, but impossibilities cannot . . . a man may, by the assistance of God's grace, keep the precepts commanded in the gospel, after such a manner, and in such a degree of perfection, as God requires of us under the denunication of eternal damnation . . . not as sinless or absolutely perfect obedience, but such as consists in a sincere love and habit of piety, which excludes all habit of sin, with all enormous and deliberate actions. . . . Besides, we do not say a man can live blameless as without falling into any sin . . . but this we do assert, that we ought to proceed in a Christian course, to amend our failings, to watch against temptations, till at last we arrive to perfection, and by the grace of God attain everlasting life.[3]

3. *Ibid.*, pp. 136ff.

8

Outstanding Mystics on Perfection

During the Reformation in Europe, there arose several outstanding mystics whose experiences, lives and testimonies present the best in the higher Christian life before Wesley's time. In this chapter we shall present several of these, together with their personal testimonies or observations of others about them.

Madam Guyon

Madam Guyon was probably converted at four years of age, but experienced various periods of relapses until about 1668, when she became more firmly established. She says of that experience: "My heart was quite changed, that God was there; for from that moment He had given me an experience of His presence in my soul. . . . I was all of a sudden so altered, that I was hardly to be known either to myself or others." She had great joy in prayer and communion, in which she spent much time, as well as doing practical Christian work for her Lord in visiting and ministering unto the poor and needy.

For about two years she enjoyed this wonderful experience, then she was drawn away to some extent into worldly conformity. Her chief temptation was in worldly dress and conversation. This brought her to deeper reflection, and created a hunger for a more victorious Christian experience.

One day she was walking across one of the bridges of the river Seine, in Paris, accompanied by her footman, on her way to Notre Dame church. A poor man in religious garb suddenly joined them and entered into religious conversation. "This man," she says, "spoke to me in a wonderful manner of God and divine things." He seemed to know all about her history, her virtues, and her faults.

She says further: "He gave me to understand that God required not merely a heart of which it could only be said it is forgiven, but a heart which could properly, and in some real sense, be designated as *holy,* that it was not sufficient to escape hell, but that he demanded also the subjection of the evils of our nature, and the utmost purity and height of Christian attainment."

Concerning her response to this conversation Madam Guyon says: "The Spirit of God bare witness to what he said. The words of this remarkable man . . . penetrated my soul. Deeply affected and overcome by what he had said, I had no sooner reached the church than I fainted away."

J. Gilchrist Lawson continues the story:

> She resolved that day before leaving the church, to give herself to the Lord anew. She resolved: "From this day, this hour, if it be possible, I will be wholly the Lord's. The world shall have no portion in me." Two years later she drew up and signed her historic Covenant of Consecration; but the real consecration seems to have been completed that day when she visited Notre Dame church. She yielded herself without reserve to the will of God, and almost immediately her consecration was tested by a series of overwhelming

> afflictions which served to purge out the dross that was in her nature. Her idols were destroyed one after another until all her hopes and joys and ambitions were centered in the Lord, and then He began to use her mightily in the building up of His kingdom.[1]

Her biographers describe the afflictions and testings that God allowed her to go through. She was stricken with smallpox which effaced her beauty; she lost her youngest son; in 1672 her beloved father died, and the same year her three-year-old daughter passed away. The death of her friend and counsellor, Genevieve Grainger, broke down another of her human props and caused her to lean more wholly on the Lord. In 1676 her husband who had become reconciled to her was taken in death.

She was enabled to see the hand of God in all these things, that He was humbling her proud heart and will, purifying her soul of dross. All this was climaxed by a seven-year period of stress which she afterwards called her "state of privation, or desolation."

Father La Combe especially helped her by his prayers and letters. She appointed the 22nd of July, 1680, as a day in which Father La Combe should pray especially for her. Although he was a long way off, her letter reached him in time, so that both of them spent the whole day in prayer and fasting. Great deliverance came to her soul. Clouds of darkness lifted and floods of glory rolled through her soul.

Of this experience she says:

> What I had possessed some years before, in the period of my spiritual enjoyment, was consolation, peace—the gift of God rather than the Giver; but now I was brought in such harmony with the will of God, that I might now be said to possess not merely consolation, but the *God* of consolation; not merely peace, but

1. Lawson, *Deeper Experiences*, pp. 97 ff.

> the *God* of peace. This true peace of mind was worth all that I had undergone, although it was only in its dawning.

Lawson quotes Madam Guyon further, from her book *Torrents*. She writes: "As a sanctified heart is always in harmony with the divine providences, I had no will but the divine will, of which such providences are the true and appropriate expression."

In another place she says: "One characteristic of this higher experience was a sense of inward purity."

Following her own encounter with God, she began to lead others into the experience of sanctification through faith. She was fond of describing it as "victory over the self life" or "death to the self life." Her soul was ablaze with the unction and power of the Holy Spirit. Everywhere she went she was besieged by multitudes of hungry, thirsty souls who flocked to her for the spiritual meat that they failed to get from their regular pastors. Revivals of religion began in almost every place she visited, and all over France earnest Christians began to seek the deeper experience taught by her.[2]

The Christian world is somewhat acquainted with the remarkable ministry of Madam Guyon, but not many realize that the source and power of that ministry was nothing less than what Wesley called entire sanctification, or Christian perfection. It is true that she approached this experience by degrees, but it is also true that there was a definite time when she exercised faith in God for immediate deliverance from inward foes. She was victorious from that hour, and looked upon it as a crisis in her religious life.

Wesley himself taught that there was usually a gradual approach to Christian perfection, and a gradual growth

---

2. *Ibid.*, pp. 102ff.

following the experience. This was exactly the case with Madam Guyon.

Bishop Fenelon

Fenelon, the devout and learned bishop of Cambray, France (1651-1715), was led by Madam Guyon into the higher experience. He also became a champion of the doctrine of "the interior life of self-crucifixion and pure love." In his book *Maxims of the Saints Concerning the Interior Life,* he showed that the most eminent saints all down through the ages had experienced and taught this doctrine, if not formally at least informally. He quoted from such outstanding characters as St. Francis of Sales, St. Francis of Assisi, John of the Cross, Father Alvarez, St. Thomas Aquinas, St. Bernard, St. Theresa, Dionysius the Areopagite, Gregory Lopez, and others.

His work, like that of Madam Guyon, encountered fierce opposition from the papacy, but it permeated France and the continent of Europe, and has continued its influence to the present day.

Fox and the Quakers

George Fox and his colaborers are often classed as among the later Mystics. Probably no other organized religious group has continued to maintain the teaching of this doctrine over so long a period of its history, and among so large a percentage of its members and leaders, as has the Friends (Quaker) Church.

Lawson writes regarding Fox,

> The Lord continued to lead him on from step to step in his Christian experience. . . . He hungered and thirsted for a deeper experience, and the Lord showed him that it was possible for him to have complete spiritual victory. He was led to see that there are two laws controlling men, the law of the flesh and the law of the

Spirit, and that through the indwelling Spirit of God the Christian should have "liberty and victory over the flesh and its works."

The one great object of all George Fox's preaching and ministry was to turn the eyes of the people away from outward forms and ceremonies, and to direct them to the need of real holiness of heart and life. And such was also the real object of the ministry of Jesus. . . . He taught them that they must be pure in heart, meek in spirit, that they must love God and their neighbor, or they would not enter the kingdom of heaven. . . . So the great mission of George Fox and the Quakers was . . . to emphasize the need of inward purity and righteousness.[3]

3. *Ibid.*, pp. 96, 101.

9

Worthies Who Prepared the Way for Wesley

A number of outstanding persons in one way or another helped to pave the way for Wesley's work. They are in that grand succession of voices all down the centuries since St. Paul who havc proclaimed the glad news of Christian perfection.

Turretin and Witsius

Among those who, during the 17th century embraced or at least approached the doctrine of Christian perfection in its evangelical sense, were two learned Presbyterian divines, Turretin and Witsius. Dr. George Peck translates from the work of Turretin on *De Perfectione Sanctificationis,* vol. 2, pp. 759-60:

> The . . . question has been brought up anew, "[Can] the law . . . be perfectly fulfilled by the regenerate, that they might open the way for good works?" . . . It is to be observed, 1st. That the question is not concerning the perfection of sincerity. . . . 2nd. It is not concerning perfection in extent. 3rd. It is not concerning comparative perfection, which is attributed to some

believers who are more advanced than others, in which sense the believers of the New Testament are called perfect. . . . 4th. It is not concerning evangelical perfection, which covers our imperfections with the garment of grace and the forbearance of the Father . . . since all those things which have been done are not imputed, while those which have not been done are pardoned, that is, covered by the righteousness of Christ, in whom we are said to be perfect. Col. 2:10. For all these kinds of perfection we acknowledge.[1]

Peck also quotes from Witsius a passage which, he says, "sounds very much like Wesley":

> It cannot, indeed, be denied that sometimes the Scripture makes mention of some who are said to be perfect even in this life. But it is to be observed that the term perfection is not always used in the same sense. For, 1st. There is the perfection of sincerity. . . . 2ndly. There is a perfection of parts; and that both subjective . . . and objective. . . . 3rdly. There is a comparative perfection ascribed to those who are advanced in knowledge, faith and sanctification, in comparison of those who are still infants and untaught. . . . 4thly. There is also an evangelical perfection. 5thly, and lastly. There is also a perfection of degrees, by which a person performs all the commands of God . . . without the least defect. . . . And this is that perfection which we deny the saints in this life, though we willingly allow them all the other kinds above mentioned. (Quoted from *Economy of the Covenants,* vol. 2, pp. 59-60.)[2]

Walter Marshall, another Presbyterian, was a fellow of New College, Oxford, and later a fellow of Winchester. In 1644, he published a book entitled *The Gospel Mystery of Sanctification Opened.* Marshall writes, "Be sure to seek for holiness of heart and life only in its due order, where God hath placed it—after union with Christ, justifi-

---

1. Peck, *Christian Perfection,* pp. 118-19.
2. *Ibid.,* pp. 121-22.

cation, and the gift of the Holy Ghost; and in that order seek it earnestly, by faith, as a very necessary part of your salvation" (Quoted in *Herald of Holiness,* May 25, 1932).

Cudworth, Lucas, and Bunyan

In a sermon before the House of Commons, the learned Cudworth, who died a short time before Wesley was born, said,

> The end of the gospel is life and perfection; it is a divine nature; it is a God-like frame, and disposition of spirit; it is to make us partakers of the image of God in righteousness and true holiness. . . . I mean by holiness, nothing else but God stamped and printed upon my soul. True holiness is always breathing upward, and fluttering toward heaven, striving to embosom itself with God.

Dr. Lucas, who died in 1715, wrote a treatise on "Religious Perfection," being the third part of his *Inquiry After Happiness* from which Wesley made an extract and included it in the 24th volume of his Christian Library. Lucas wrote:

> Religion is nothing else but the purifying and refining nature by grace, the raising and exalting our faculties and capacities by wisdom and virtue. Religious perfection, therefore, is nothing else but the moral accomplishment of human nature; such a maturity of virtue as man in this life is capable of; conversion begins, perfection consummates the habit of righteousness: in the one religion is as it were in its infancy; in the other, in its strength and manhood; so that perfection, in short, is nothing else but a ripe and settled habit of true holiness. . . .
>
> The doctrine of infused habits has been much ridiculed and exposed, as absurd, by some men. . . . But why God cannot produce in us those strong dispositions to virtue in a moment, which are ordinarily produced by time; or why we may not ascribe as much efficiency to infused habits, as philosophers are wont to do to repeated acts, I cannot see. Nor can I see why such

dispositions, when infused, may not be called habits, if they have all the properties and effects of a habit.

John Bunyan was a Baptist. According to J. A. McDonald, in Bunyan's immortal *Pilgrim's Progress* he represents the work of sanctification at the "Interpreter's House." He quotes regarding "The Bath of Sanctification,"

> The Interpreter would have them tarry a while . . . take them and have them into the garden to the bath, and there wash them, and make them clean from the soil which they have gathered by traveling. Then is described by Bunyan the putting on them of a seal, of white linen garments, how they shone so brightly that "they seemed to be a terror one to the other; for that they could not see that glory each one had in himself, which they could see in each other." Now, therefore, they began to esteem each other better than themselves.[3]

To the same point is Bishop J. Paul Taylor's citation of Bunyan's experience:

> The celebrated Pilgrim after various fortunes and misfortunes arrived "in the country of Beulah," and he with his companions "heard continually the singing birds, and saw every day the flowers appear in the earth. . . . In this country the sun shineth day and night." Here they were "also out of reach of Giant Despair; neither could they from this place so much as see Doubting Castle." Here they were within sight of the City they were going to, also here met them some of the inhabitants thereof; for in this land the Shining Ones commonly walked, because it was upon the borders of heaven. In this land also the contract between the bride and Bridegroom was renewed. . . .
>
> Here they had no want of corn and wine; for in this place they met with abundance of what they had sought for in all their pilgrimage. . . . Here all the inhabitants of the country called them "the holy people";

3. McDonald, *Shorter Catechism*, pp. 93-94.

"the redeemed of the Lord." . . . As they walked in this land they had more rejoicing than in parts more remote from the Kingdom to which they were bound; and drawing near to the City, "they had yet a more perfect view thereof." . . . It is regretable that the dreamer did not discover the land of Beulah at an earlier stage of the journey and save his pilgrim from some aberrations and near-disasters to which the unsanctified are always exposed" (Quoted in the *Free Methodist,* Dec. 4, 1931).

Taylor, Kempis, Law

The men who probably influenced Wesley most in arriving at the doctrine of Christian perfection he gives credit to in the introduction of his classic *A Plain Account of Christian Perfection.*

1. What I purpose in the following paper is, to give a plain and distinct account of the steps by which I was led, during a course of many years, to embrace the doctrine of Christian perfection:

2. In the year 1725, being in the twenty-third year of my age, I met with Bishop Taylor's *Rules and Exercises of Holy Living and Dying!* . . . Instantly I resolved to dedicate all my life to God, all my thoughts, and words, and actions. . . .

3. In the year 1726, I met with Kempis' *Christian's Pattern.* The nature and extent of inward religion, the religion of the heart, now appeared to me in a stronger light than ever it had done before. I saw that giving even all my life to God . . . would profit me nothing, unless I gave my heart, yea, all my heart to him. I saw that "simplicity of intention, and purity of affection," one design in all that we speak or do, and one desire ruling all our tempers, are indeed "the wings of the soul," without which she can never ascend to the mount of God.

4. A year or two after, Mr. Law's *Christian Pattern* and *Serious Call* were put into my hands. These convinced me more than ever, of the absolute impossibility of being half a Christian; and I determined,

through his grace, (the absolute necessity of which I was deeply sensible,) to be all devoted to God, to give him all my soul, my body, and my substance. . . .

5. In the year 1729, I began not only to read, but to study, the Bible, as the one, the only standard of truth, and the only model of true religion. Hence I saw, in a clearer and clearer light, the indispensable necessity of having "the mind which was in Christ," and of "walking as Christ also walked;" even of having, not some part only, but all the mind which was in him; and of walking as he walked, not only in many or most respects, but in all things. . . .

6. On January 1, 1733, I preached before the university, in St. Mary's church, on "the circumcision of the heart," an account of which I gave in these words: It is that habitual disposition of soul which, in the sacred writings, is termed holiness; and which directly implies the being cleansed from sin, "from all filthiness both of flesh and spirit," and, by consequence, the being endued with those virtues which were in Christ; the being so "renewed in the image of our mind" as to be "perfect as our Father which is in heaven is perfect."[4]

Mr. Wesley further says:

In the same sermon I observed, "Love is the fulfilling of the law, the end of the commandment." It is not only "the first and great" command, but all the commandments in one. "Whatsoever things are just, whatsoever things are pure, if there be any virtue, if there be any praise," they are all comprised in this one word, love. In this is perfection, and glory, and happiness: the royal law of heaven and earth is this, "Thou shalt love the Lord thy God with all thy heart, and with all thy soul, and with all thy mind, and with all thy strength." . . .

It may be observed, this sermon was composed the first of all my writings which have been published. This was the view of religion I then had, which even then I scrupled not to call *perfection*. This is the view I

4. John Wesley, *Works*, 1:148.

have of it now, without any material addition or diminution. . . .

In the same sentiment did my brother and I remain (with all those young gentlemen in derision termed *Methodists*) till we embarked for America, in the latter end of 1735. . . .

In August following [in 1738], I had a long conversation with Arvid Gradin, in Germany. After he had given me an account of his experience, I desired him to give me, in writing, a definition of "the full assurance of faith," which he did in the following words:—[we omit the Latin version and give merely the English translation,] "Repose in the blood of Christ; a firm confidence in God, and persuasion of his favour; the highest tranquility, serenity, and peace of mind, with a deliverance from every fleshly desire, and a cessation of all, even inward sins."

This was the first account I ever heard from any living man, of what I had before learned from the oracles of God, and had been praying for, (with the little company of my friends,) and expecting, for several years.

In 1739, my brother and I published a volume of "Hymns and Sacred Poems." In many of these we declared our sentiments strongly and explicitly. . . .

The first tract I ever wrote expressly on this subject was published in the latter end of this year. That none might be prejudiced before they read it, I gave it the indifferent title of "The Character of a Methodist." In this I described a perfect Christian, placing in the front, "Not as though I had already attained." Part of it I subjoin without any alteration:

A Methodist is one who loves the Lord his God with all his heart, with all his soul, with all his mind, and with all his strength. . . . Perfect love having cast out fear, he rejoices evermore. . . . He loves his enemies, yea, and the enemies of God. . . . For he is "pure in heart." Love has purified his heart from envy, malice, wrath, and every unkind temper. It has cleansed him from pride, whereof "only comest contention;" and he hath now "put on bowels of mercies, kindness, humbleness of mind, meekness, long suffering." And indeed all possible ground for contention, on his part, is cut off. . . .

All the commandments of God he accordingly keeps, and that with all his might; for his obedience is in proportion to his love, the source from whence it flows. And, therefore, loving God with all his heart, he serves him with all his strength. . . . All the talents he has, he constantly employs according to his Master's will; every power and faculty of his soul, every member of his body.

These are the very words wherein I largely declared, for the first time, my sentiments of Christian perfection. And is it not easy to see, (1) That this is the very point at which I aimed all along from the year 1725; and more determinately from the year 1730. . . . (2) That this is the very same doctrine which I believe and teach at this day; not adding one point, either to that inner or outward holiness which I maintained eight and thirty years ago.

I do not know that any writer has made any objection against that tract to this day; and for some time I did not find much opposition upon the head, at least, not from serious persons. But, after a time, a cry arose. . . .

I think it was in the latter end of the year 1740, that I had a conversation with Dr. Gibson, then bishop of London, at Whitehall. He asked me what I meant by perfection. I told him without any disguise or reserve. When I ceased speaking, he said, "Mr. Wesley, if this be all you mean, publish it to all the world. If any one then can confute what you say, he may have free leave." I answered, "My Lord, I will," and accordingly wrote and published the sermon on Christian perfection.[5]

---

5. *Ibid.*

10

Effect of the Moravian Pentecost on Wesley

A group of Moravian missionaries on the boat with Wesley on his trip to Georgia were the first who bore witness to him of salvation by faith.

By Wesley's time, the Reformation had drifted far back toward Catholicism and salvation by works. Wesley had fled the shores of England in the hope of saving his soul by getting away from the evil temptations there, and by working to convert the heathen Indians. His mission there had ended in miserable failure, and he returned to England, almost on the brink of despair. He feared that he might never find that peace with God which he sought. It was a Moravian, Peter Bohler, who showed him the way to salvation by faith alone.

A fiery Pentecostal baptism of the Holy Spirit had fallen upon a comparatively weak and diverse group of Christians at Herrnhut, Germany, August 13, 1727. From those Spirit-filled Christians came this group of Moravian missionaries. They were now on their way to Georgia to witness to both white men and Indians of the mighty power of God that saves and redeems men. This Pentecostal baptism had transformed that small group of Christians into fiery evangelists, whose influence spread eventually to the uttermost parts of the earth. This Pentecostal baptism also resulted in the rebirth and remaking of the Moravian Church. Immediately they began to send forth missionaries 50 years before the dawn of the great foreign missionary era under William Carey of India. This Pentecost was in part instrumental in John and Charles Wesley's establishment in the faith and was the inspiration of a wealth of Christian hymns.

Count Zinzendorf, the leader of the Moravians, and his followers, never advanced the doctrine of Christian perfection as a crisis experience as afterwards formulated by John Wesley. Their experience at Herrnhut, however, was certainly similar to, if not identical with, the experience of entire sanctification taught by Wesley and experienced by multitudes of the Methodists.

Rev. John Greenfield, of Warsaw, Ind., has written an interesting account of the Moravian Pentecost. It was prepared for the 200th anniversary observance by the Moravians of that momentous event.

> We are now celebrating the Bi-Centennial of what our Moravian Textbook calls the "Signal out-pouring of the Holy Spirit experienced by the congregation of Herrnhut." . . . A Moravian historian writes . . . as follows: "God Says: 'It shall come to pass—I will pour.' This was His promise through the prophet Joel. The first fulfillment of this promise was on the day of Pentecost. There is nothing in the New Testament to indicate that this was to be the one and only fulfillment of this promise. . . . Church history also abounds in records of special outpourings of the Holy Ghost, and verily the thirteenth of August, 1727, was a day of the outpouring of the Holy Spirit. We saw the hand of God and his wonders, and we were all under the cloud of our fathers baptized with their spirit. The Holy Ghost

came upon us and in those days great signs and wonders took place in our midst. From that time scarcely a day passed but what we beheld His almighty workings amongst us. A great hunger after the Word of God took possession of us so that we had to have three services every day. . . . Everyone desired above everything else that the Holy Spirit might have full control. Self-love and self-will as well as all disobedience disappeared and an overwhelming flood of grace swept us all out into the great ocean of Divine Love."

Exactly what happened that Wednesday forenoon, August 13th, 1727, in the specially called Communion service at Berthelsdorf, none of the participants could fully describe. They left the house of God that noon "hardly knowing whether they belonged to earth or had already gone to Heaven."[1]

Greenfield quotes from a summary by Bishop Edward Rondthaler:

> Zinzendorf, who gives us the deepest and most vivid account of this wonderful occurrence, says it was "a sense of the nearness of Christ" bestowed in a single moment upon all the members that were present: and it was so unanimous that two members, at work twenty miles away, unaware that the meeting was being held, became at the same time, deeply conscious of the same blessing.
>
> These members were all laity, though at a later time, ministers and missionaries, deacons, presbyters and bishops arose out of the wonderfully blessed assemblage. . . .
>
> It was a young congregation which received the 13th of August blessing. Zinzendorf, the human leader, was just twenty-seven years old, and if a census had been taken, it would have been found that his own age was approximately the average of the whole company.[2]

The spiritual experiences of the Moravian brethren two centuries ago bear a striking resemblance to the Pente-

---

1. John Greenfield, *Power from on High*, pp. 9-11.
2. *Ibid.*, pp. 11-12.

costal power and results in the days of the apostles. The company of believers both at Jerusalem and Herrnhut numbered less than 300 souls. Both congregations were devoid of worldly influence, wisdom, power, and wealth. At once these believers, naturally timid and fearful, were transformed into flaming evangelists. Supernatural knowledge and power seemed to possess them.

During the first three decades after their spiritual Pentecost at Herrnhut, the Moravians carried the gospel of salvation, not only to nearly every country in Europe but also to many pagan races in North America, South America, Asia, and Africa.

Greenfield describes the unpromising condition of the company at Herrnhut with their differences of opinion and heated controversy on doctrinal questions before this outpouring of the Spirit. He also relates how Count Zinzendorf prepared them for this enduement.

> The first part of the year 1727 did not seem very promising. Differences of opinion and heated controversy on doctrinal questions threatened to disrupt the congregation. The majority were members of the Ancient Moravian Church of the Brethren. But other believers had also been attracted to Herrnhut. Lutherans, Reformed, Baptists, etc., had joined the community. Questions of predestination, holiness, the meaning and mode of baptism, etc., seemed likely to divide the believers into a number of small and belligerent sects. Then the more earnest and spiritual souls among them began to cry mightily unto the Lord for deliverance. His first answer was a general outpouring upon them of "the spirit of grace and supplication" (Zech. 12:10). . . .
>
> He also sent them a human leader and deliverer in the person of the young German nobleman, Count Zinzendorf, who so kindly had offered this persecuted church a place of refuge on his own estates. This godly youth and pre-eminent genius had been divinely prepared for his great work of spiritual leadership. . . . Count Zinzendorf had early learned the secret of

prevailing prayer. So active had he been in establishing circles for prayer, that on leaving the college at Halle, sixteen years of age, he handed the famous Professor Francke a list of seven praying societies. . . . It was a condition and not a theory which confronted the young nobleman in 1727 at Herrnhut. How to unite in faith and love and service the pious but disputatious followers of Huss, Luther, Calvin, Zwingle, Schwenkfeld, etc., seemed indeed a hopeless problem apart from divine intervention. In answer to earnest and persevering prayer superhuman wisdom guided the young Count in the use of certain means which proved of incalculable value.[3]

Bishop J. T. Hamilton has called attention to this in a recent article in the *Moravian*. He describes the Brotherly Covenant drawn up by Zinzendorf calling upon them "to seek out and emphasize the points in which they agreed" rather than to stress their differences. He also tells of the count's personal interview with every individual adult resident in Herrnhut. Bishop Hamilton says:

> But far more important than this was their entering into solemn covenant with Zinzendorf, that twelfth of May, to actually dedicate their lives, as he dedicated his, to the service of the Lord Jesus Christ, each one in his particular calling and position. This covenant was in essentials what constitutes our Brotherly Agreement of today. . . .
>
> There followed the choice of the twelve elders to complete the organization of the spiritual life of Herrnhut, and the appointment of persons to the various offices foreseen in the statutes. So order, itself a product of greater mutual confidence as well as of mutually recognized devotion, made possible provision for the Bible study and the frequent gathering of bands for prayer, that next marked the ensuing summer months and led the way to and prepared the way for the baptism of the Spirit that culminated on that blessed thirteenth of August, an enduement with power, that

3. *Ibid.*, pp. 19-21.

enabled those men and women of Herrnhut to serve their generation so effectively.[4]

The great Moravian revival of 1727, which reached its climax August 13, was preceded and followed by most extraordinary praying. The spirit of grace and supplications manifested itself in the early part of the year. Count Zinzendorf had begun to give spiritual instructions to a class of nine girls between the ages of 10 and 13 years. The historian of that period tells us, "The Count frequently complained to his consort that though the children behaved with great outward propriety, he could not perceive any traces of spiritual life among them; and however much might be said to them of the Lord Jesus Christ, yet it did not seem to reach their hearts."

In this distress of mind he took his burden to the Lord in prayer, most fervently asking God to grant to these children His grace and blessing. What a spectacle! A gifted, wealthy, young German nobleman on his knees, agonizing in prayer for the conversion of some schoolgirls!

On July 16, the Count poured forth his soul in a heart-affecting prayer, accompanied with a flood of tears. This prayer produced an extraordinary effect, and was the beginning of the subsequent operation of the Spirit of God. Not only Count Zinzendorf, but many others also began to pray as never before.

In the "Memorial Days of the Renewed Moravian Church," we read as follows:

> July 22. A number of Brethren covenanted together of their own accord, engaging to meet often on the Hutberg, to pour out their hearts in prayer and hymns.
>
> On the fifth of August the Warden, viz., the Count, spent the whole night in watching, in company of about twelve or fourteen brethren. At mid-night there was

4. *Ibid.*, p. 22.

held on the Hutberg a large meeting for the purpose of prayer, at which great emotion prevailed.

On Sunday, August 10, about noon, while Pastor Rothe was holding the meeting at Herrnhut, he felt himself overwhelmed by a wonderful and irresistible power of the Lord, and sunk down into the dust before God, and with him sunk down the whole assembled congregation, in an ecstacy of feeling. In this frame of mind they continued until midnight engaged in prayer and singing, weeping and supplication.

After that distinguished day of blessing, the 13th day of August, 1727, the thought struck some brethren and sisters that it might be well to set apart certain hours for the purpose of prayer, at which seasons all might be reminded of its excellency, and be induced by the promise annexed to fervent prayer to pour out their hearts before the Lord.

It was moreover considered as an important point that, as in the days of the Old Covenant, the sacred fire was never permitted to go out on the altar (Lev. 6:13 and 14), so in a congregation which is a temple of the living God, wherein He has His altar and His fire, the intercession of His saints should incessantly rise up unto Him like holy incense.

On August 26 twenty-four brethren and the same number of sisters met, and covenanted together to continue from one midnight to the next in prayer, dividing for that purpose the twenty-four hours of night and day by lot among themselves.

August 27 this new regulation was put into practice. More were soon added to this number of intercessors, which was thus increased to seventy-seven, and even the awakened children began a plan similar to this among themselves. Everyone carefully observed the hour which had been appointed for them. The intercessors had a weekly meeting, at which notice was given them of those things which they were to consider special subjects for prayer and remembrance before the Lord.

The children of both sexes felt a most powerful impulse to prayer, and it was impossible to listen to their infant supplications without being deeply moved and affected. A blessed meeting of the children took place in the evening of the 26th of August, and on the 29th, from the hours of ten o'clock at night until one the following morning a truly affecting scene was witnessed for the girls of Herrnhut and Berthelsdorf spent these hours in praying, singing and weeping on the Hutberg. The boys were at the same time engaged in earnest prayer in another place. The spirit of prayer and supplication at that time poured out upon the children was so powerful and efficacious that it is impossible to give an adequate description of it in words. These were truly days of heavenly enjoyment to the congregation at Herrnhut; all forgot themselves, and things terrestrial and transitory, and longed to be above with Christ, in bliss everlasting.[5]

Another eyewitness says:

I cannot ascribe the cause of the great awakening of the children at Herrnhut to anything but the wonderful outpouring of the Spirit of God upon the communicant congregation assembled on that occasion. The breezes of the Spirit pervaded at that time equally both young and old.

Again we quote from Bishop Evelyn Hasse:

Was there ever in the whole of church history such an astonishing prayer-meeting as that which beginning in 1727, went on one hundred years. It is something absolutely unique. It was known as the "Hourly Intercession", and it meant that by relays of Brethren and Sisters prayer without ceasing was made to God for all the work and wants of His church. Prayer of that kind always leads to action. In this case it kindled a burning desire to make Christ's Salvation known to the heathen. It led to the beginning of Foreign Missions. From that one small village community more than one hundred missionaries went out in twenty-five years. You will look in vain elsewhere for anything to match it in anything like the same extent.[6]

---

5. *Ibid.*
6. *Ibid.*, pp. 25-26.

Despite this remarkable experience the Moravians did not formulate a particular doctrine of Christian perfection. They did, however, teach what they called, "The full assurance of faith," which Arvid Gradin, one of their leaders defined to Wesley, in the following words: "Repose in the blood of Christ; a firm confidence in God, and persuasion in his favour; the highest tranquility, serenity, and peace of mind, with a deliverance from every fleshly desire, and a cessation of all, even inward sins."

This was not the experience of the Moravians before August 13, 1727, but it was their experience after that outpouring of the Spirit. Wesley apparently equated the Moravian outpouring and doctrine with his own teaching of entire sanctification. Referring to Gradin's definition of "the full assurance of faith," he says: "That was the first account I ever heard from any living man, of what I had before learned myself from the oracles of God, and had been praying for, (with the little company of my friends,) and expecting for several years." Beyond doubt, this Moravian Pentecost experience in the church of that day brought Mr. Wesley to consider more seriously than he had done before the evidences for Christian perfection from the past centuries. It confirmed his conviction that such an experience as had happened to the Herrnhut Christians was a normal expectation for all born-again believers in this age.

Out of these convictions and his understanding of the Word of God, John Wesley went forward to stress this experience. He formulated the doctrine of Christian perfection more fully, and sought to focus interest in this experience and doctrine by the Christians of his times.

As we have traced the doctrines of the Old and New Testaments on the subject of Christian perfection, and looked at the lives, experiences, and teachings of the saints through the centuries, it seems clear that Wesley's idea was not a new one. Rather, here was a doctrine and an experience founded solidly upon the Word of God and sustained by the testimony of the Christian Church ever since the time of the apostle Paul.

11

From Wesley to the 20th Century

This chapter does not labor to establish the position of Mr. Wesley, nor to give a detailed history of the movement of Christian perfection since his time. Rather, we give a brief outline of the progress made during these two centuries, and highlight the churches and leaders who have been active in this progress.

It may be noted that no church doctrine was fully set forth in apostolic times in systematic form. Rather, doctrine grew through the ages as the Church's need demanded such formulations of her teachings. As we have seen, it was as late as the days of Wesley before any very clear statement of the doctrine of regeneration was made. Although Luther had defined and greatly expanded the doctrine of justification by faith, as it formed the main bulwark of his Reformation thrust, he did not develop the related doctrine of regeneration. This was done more successfully by Mr. Wesley than by anyone before him. He and his immediate followers also elaborated and established the doctrine of Christian perfection more fully than had been done since apostolic times.

Sanctification by faith for the believer already "in Christ" was Mr. Wesley's main doctrinal contribution to the progress of the Church. He saw that it had been a neglected truth and therefore strove to more sharply define and establish this particular doctrine. More than any man since St. Paul's time, Wesley held up Christian perfection as the ideal goal of all Christian believers, as a possible attainment in this life. And God raised up a multitude of witnesses in his days who testified to the truth of both the experience and the doctrine.

The most able exponents of holiness doctrine besides Wesley in his own time were John Fletcher, one of his ablest co-workers; and, a bit later, Dr. Adam Clarke, the great Scripture commentator. Perhaps the best known works of Fletcher are his *Christian Perfection,* and *Checks to Antinomianism.* The latter is by far his greatest contribution to Wesleyan theology.

Following Wesley's time, came Dr. W. B. Pope's *Compendium of Christian Theology.* It became a standard theological work of early Methodism with its clear statement of Christian holiness. Mention should also be made of George D. Watson's *Love Abounding,* and a score of smaller holiness books.

The Wesleyan message soon spread to young America, where it began to take hold among the colonists. In Wesley's last days, Thomas Coke was sent by him to be the first bishop of Methodism in America, but Coke did not succeed to any great degree. Bishop Francis Asbury was consecrated the first American Bishop of Methodism in the United States. He was far more successful than the Englishman, Coke.

In these early times the message of Christian perfection was interwoven into the Methodist evangelical appeal to the masses. As the work continued to grow and spread, this message was also made plain as part of the Methodist church's heritage.

Charles G. Finney and Asa Mahan were among the first Americans in the Calvinist tradition to receive the second crisis experience of the baptism with the Spirit. Finney received this mighty baptism soon after his conversion and became a flaming evangel who won tens of thousands to God. Asa Mahan was a scholar who did much to turn the American Calvinistic tide in theology back toward the more biblical position of Arminianism.[1]

As Methodism spread in this country, the camp meeting institution sprang up in Kentucky and Tennessee, then spread westward and eastward as it fanned out. The Presbyterians actually established the open air meeting. But when the Methodists saw in it a good opportunity for soul winning, they flocked to the camps of the Presbyterians in great numbers. The Methodists, with their shouting and emotionalism, crowded the more staid Presbyterians from the field. Though without deliberate intent, the Methodists took over the field and developed the camp meeting into a great institution that spread the flame of evangelism in many sections of this country.

As Methodism spread and enlarged, there came a declining emphasis on the doctrine and experience of Christian perfection. Out of this drift a deep concern arose in many sections of Methodism that the message of Christian holiness be not lost. Several groups pulled out of the church while others chose to remain and tackle the problem from within.

The rise of the Quaker movement in England almost 100 years before Wesley's time, resulted in the Friends

---

1. See Turner, *Vision,* p. 301.

Church. There have been and are diversities in their congregations and some have neglected the message of Christian perfection. But others have remained true to the message. The Yearly Meetings of the Evangelical Friends cling to the pure and unadulterated message as Fox and Wesley taught it.

The Salvation Army

Around 1865 William Booth and his wife, Catherine, began street preaching in London. About the year 1880 this eventuated in the organization of the Salvation Army. This work grew into a worldwide ministry and in many instances has carried the message of Christian perfection faithfully to its listeners. The doctrine of entire sanctification has been one of the cardinal tenets of the Salvation Army, and the organization has been among the main supporters of the Christian Holiness Association.

The Wesleyan Church

In the 1840s a group of earnest Methodists in New York banded together to fight against slavery and to work for its abolition. The Methodist church as a denomination, had at this time taken no serious stand against slavery, although many individual Methodists were opposed to it. As time passed, this group stirred up considerable opposition within the Methodist church. In addition to the slavery issue, they had also adopted as part of their determined stand the challenge to help keep alive the doctrine of Christian perfection. Ministers Lee and Scott, among others, emerged as the leaders in this movement. In 1845, they separated from the Methodist church and formed what was known as the Wesleyan Methodist Connection, later called the Wesleyan Methodist Church. In 1968, they and the Pilgrim Holiness Church united to form The Wesleyan Church. They have been staunch supporters of the doctrine of Christian perfection for nearly a century and a half.

The Christian Holiness Association

Around 1850-60 there arose in several denominations groups of devout people interested in seeing the doctrine and experience of Christian holiness promoted. Phoebe Palmer and many of her associates, while silent on the issue of slavery, were quite vocal on the matter of sanctification. Out of these meetings and discussion groups finally grew the National Association for the Promotion of Holiness. By the mid-twentieth century this association had shortened its name to the National Holiness Association. Later, because its program was international in scope, and also to sharpen the focus of its message, the name Christian Holiness Association was adopted. Its major thrust has always been the promotion of the message of Christian perfection and its practical applications in missions, education, and social concerns.[2]

The Free Methodist Church

Prior to 1860, Rev. B. T. Roberts and others had carried on an effective ministry within the Methodist church for a return to the purity and simplicity that had characterized early Methodism. This attempted revival did not seriously affect the general body of Methodists but won many converts to its cause especially in New York and Michigan. These men also contended for free pews for everyone, against the standard custom of renting pews to the families of the church. For their strong stand against these practices, they were expelled from the church. After seeking restoration without success, Roberts and others finally organized at Pekin, N.Y., August 23, 1860, what was

---

2. *Ibid.*, pp. 314 ff.

known as the Free Methodist Church. The term "Free" signified that this church would offer to all attendants free pews, refusing to follow the then current Methodist practice of renting pews to raise church money. The doctrine of Christian perfection was prominent in this church from its inception, and has remained so to this time. The Free Methodists have a worldwide ministry in missions and education, with a constituency of around 200,000.

The Pilgrim Holiness Church

In 1897, in Cincinnati, Ohio, Martin Wells Knapp and Seth Rees formed, with others, a small group that became known as the International Apostolic Holiness Union and Churches. The name was later changed to the International Holiness Church. In 1922 Seth Rees brought a group known as the Pilgrim Church which he had organized in California, to unite with the International Holiness Church. The Pilgrim Holiness Church resulted from this merger. This group has been a faithful carrier of the Christian perfection message through all its history. The Pilgrims and the Wesleyan Methodists had developed similar missionary programs. They also had much in common doctrinally and in size of membership and constituency were quite parallel. After several years of negotiations these two bodies merged in 1968 to form The Wesleyan Church. Together their worldwide constituency stands at over 300,000.

The Church of the Nazarene

The Church of the Nazarene, with international headquarters in Kansas City, Mo., is the largest denomination which carries the banner of Christian perfection as one of its cardinal doctrines. This group had its organizational origins around the turn of the century.

In the booklet *Introducing the Nazarenes,* Leslie Parrott has given the most important facts concerning the rise of this body of believers as a denomination. Dr. P. F. Bresee was pastor of the First Methodist Church of Los Angeles, Calif., and later of the Methodist Church in Pasadena. He had such a successful ministry that at the end of his second year a tabernacle seating 2,000 was erected to care for the congregation's growing needs.

Dr. Bresee was a strong preacher of righteousness and a staunch advocate of entire sanctification. He did not hesitate to preach the doctrine and witness to this experience. Not all within Methodism in southern California were happy with this ministry. Parrott says of him, "Resistence from the hierarchy, his desire to serve the poor, a feeling that Methodism in southern California had turned the corner away from the tide of holiness evangelism, and an unquestioned personal commitment to the Spirit-filled life, were key factors in the push-and-pull of Dr. Bresee's decision to seek a 'supernumerary relation' with the Methodist church."

But Bresee did not long remain out of the center of things for the cause of holiness. On October 6, 1895, he was preaching to a group of people in a rented hall in Los Angeles. Two weeks later he organized the first Church of the Nazarene with 86 initial members (135 by the time the charter was closed). A piece of Nazarene literature printed about this time declared that this new body was "a church of the people and for the people. . . . Its mission is to everyone upon whom the battle of life has been sore, and to every heart that hungers for cleansing from sin."

The southern California movement had counterparts elsewhere in the nation, where both ministers and laymen had been ostracized from the older churches for their determination to hold fast to the doctrine of Christian perfection. One such group from the Northeast joined Bresee and his group in a special union meeting in Chicago, in 1907. The following year a similar group from the South joined forces with them at a uniting assembly at Pilot Point, Tex. As Parrott writes, "Here in a small community northwest of Dallas, on October 13, 1908, the Church of the Nazarene officially joined the family of denominations who follow the succession from the Cross through the ministries of Augustine, Luther, Arminius, and the Wesleys."

From a small beginning, this church has grown until today it has almost 6,800 churches, with nearly 550 missionaries working in more than 50 countries around the world. The church ministers to about 1,250,000 pupils in its Sunday schools and reaches a constituency of perhaps 2,000,000.

The message of Christian perfection still permeates sections of the Methodist church. Such schools as Asbury College, and Asbury Seminary, Wilmore, Ky.; and Taylor University, Upland, Ind., are Methodist schools that stress the Wesleyan message.

A large majority of Asbury Seminary graduates, and many more graduates from Asbury College are placed in Methodist pastorates annually. In spite of official silence concerning the doctrine, the holiness message is still proclaimed from many Methodist pulpits. Such great camp meetings as Camp Sychar, in Ohio, Indian Springs in Georgia, and Romeo in Michigan, further testify that the message of sanctification is still very much alive in Methodism.

To be acquainted with the many providences which have made possible the preservation of the message of heart holiness through the centuries, is to have a deeper appreciation for its significance. From this background comes a better understanding of what we believe and why concerning this doctrine. The Bible speaks clearly to every follower of Christ: "This is the will of God, even your sanctification" (1 Thess. 4:3). And again, "The very God of peace sanctify you wholly; and I pray God your whole spirit and soul and body be preserved blameless unto the coming of our Lord Jesus Christ. Faithful is he that calleth you, who also will do it" (1 Thess. 5:23-24).

Bibliography

The Ante-Nicene Fathers. Grand Rapids: Baker Book House, n.d.

Cassaway, B. F., *Entire Sanctification,* from Wesley's Journals. Louisville, Ky.: Pentecostal Publishing Company.

Clarke, Adam, *Commentary on the Holy Bible.* Nashville: Abingdon-Cokesbury Press, n.d.

Deal, Wm. S., *Heart Talks on the Deeper Life.* Winona Lake, Ind.: Higley-Huffman Press, 1952.

Fletcher, John, *Christian Perfection.* Louisville, Ky.: Pentecostal Publishing Co., n.d.

Greenfield, John, *Power from on High.* Warsaw, Ind.: John Greenfield, n.d.

Henschen, Walter G., *Christian Perfection Before Wesley.* Apollo, Pa.: West Publishing Company, 1952.

Lake, Kirsopp, *The Apostolic Fathers.* New York: The Macmillan Co., 1912.

Lawson, J. Gilchrist, *Deeper Experiences of Famous Christians.* Anderson, Ind.: The Warner Press, 1911.

McDonald, James A., *Wesley's Revision of the Shorter Catechism.* (Nodata).

Peck, George, *The Scripture Doctrine of Christian Perfection.* New York: Lane and Scott, 1850.

Pope, W. B., *A Compendium of Christian Theology.* 3 vols. Nashville: The Methodist Publishing House, n.d.

Strong, H. A., *Systematic Theology.* Philadelphia: Westminster Press, n.d.

Turner, George Allen, *The Vision Which Transforms.* Kansas City, Mo.: Beacon Hill Press of Kansas City, 1964.

Wesley, John, *Standard Sermons.* Nashville: The Methodist Publishing House, 1923.

———, *Journals of John Wesley.* London: Epworth Press, 1938.

———, *A Plain Account of Christian Perfection.* Kansas City: Beacon Hill Press of Kansas City, 1966.

———, *Letters of John Wesley.* John Telford, editor. 8 vols. London: The Epworth Press, 1931.

———, *Works of John Wesley.* (Reprint) 14 vols. Grand Rapids: Zondervan Publishing House, n.d.

Wimberly, C. F. *Beacon Lights of Faith.* New York: Fleming H. Revell Co., 1929.

Wood, J. A., *Purity and Maturity.* Chicago: Christian Witness Company, 1899.